A Senator's Wife Remembers

ALSO BY HENRIETTA McCORMICK HILL

The Family Skeleton (1958)

A SENATOR'S WIFE REMEMBERS

From the Great Depression to the Great Society

HENRIETTA McCORMICK HILL

NEWSOUTH BOOKS
Montgomery | Louisville

NewSouth Books
105 S. Court Street
Montgomery, AL 36104

Library of Congress Cataloging-in-Publication Data

Hill, Henrietta McCormick, b. 1904.
A senator's wife remembers : from the Great Depression to the Great Society /
Henrietta McCormick Hill.
p. cm.

ISBN-13: 978-1-60306-056-1
ISBN-10: 1-60306-056-1

1. Hill, Henrietta McCormick, b. 1904. 2. Hill, Lister, 1894-1984. 3.
Legislators' spouses—United States—Biography. 4. Legislators—United States—
Biography. 5. United States. Congress. House—Biography. 6. United States.
Congress. Senate—Biography. 7. United States—Politics and government—
20th century. 8. Politicians' spouses—Alabama—Biography.
9. Politicians—Alabama—Biography. I. Title.
E748.H545H55 2010
328.73'092—dc22
[B]

2010016314

Printed in the United States of America

Published by Henrietta H. Hubbard in loving memory of my mother,
Henrietta McCormick Hill. On her original manuscript, my mother
inscribed these words:

THIS BOOK IS DEDICATED TO LISTER HILL, THE MAN WITH WHOM
I SHARED THOSE YEARS. ON FEBRUARY 20, 1968, LISTER AND I
CELEBRATED OUR FORTIETH WEDDING ANNIVERSARY.

Contents

12 pages of photographs follow page 144

Foreword

My mother, Henrietta McCormick Hill, waited a number of years after the 1956 death of her own mother, Henrietta [Etta] Copeland McCormick Dent, to open a box labeled "Henrietta's letters, for her book."

Like mother, like daughter. It has taken me twenty-one years since my mother's death in 1986 to rediscover a box I had forgotten in the attic. It was our 2004 move to Midlane Court in Montgomery that revealed it to me again. In this box were a number of letters my mother had written to her mother and to her husband, Joseph Lister Hill. Also in that box were her diaries, kept over most of her lifetime.

More importantly, I found three manuscripts my mother had written, culled from these letters and journal entries. These manuscripts were drafts of her "book" which she had been unable to finish due to her eventual incapacitation from Parkinson's disease.

I felt called upon to try to get her "book" edited and published. In 1958 my mother self-published a book entitled *The Family Skeleton*; that book contained mainly family stories and genealogical charts tracing her ancestry. This other book, however, contains insights into her era and society that I think will be of interest to many.

My mother, her mother, and I were very close and shared many family memories while sitting on my grandmother's front porch after supper in Eufaula, Alabama. In these pages, I hope the glow of those evenings will be shared with you.

Montgomery, Alabama
April 2010

Preface

HENRIETTA McCORMICK HILL

T oday is a rainy day with a penetrating cold which chills the marrow. Just the kind of a day one cleans out the trunk closet and does the little chores saved for such a time.

I am sitting on the floor of my bedroom in Washington, surrounded by stacks of old letters. This is the first time I have had the courage to open the box in which these letters have been stored for the past many years. I found them in back of Mother's [Henrietta Copeland McCormick Dent] closet when we were clearing out her personal effects after her funeral in 1956. The large carton that contained these letters had a message to me written on top: "Henrietta's letters, for her book." Now why did Mama do that to me?

I wrote these letters to my mother during the time in which I lived in Washington. They are poorly written, most of them scribbled in a hurry. The letters start in 1928 when I was a new bride of two months. I was then twenty-three years old. Lister and I were living at the Washington Hotel. [Other entries in this book come from a various sources, including journal excerpts and original newspaper articles.]

Life was new and strange. Of politics I knew nothing. Of the social customs of Official Washington, I was entirely ignorant. Old timers warned me that I must never, under any circumstances, precede the wife of anyone who outranked my husband; I could never leave a party until all of the people who outranked me had said goodbye. I was informed that I was to leave visiting cards at the White House, at the home of the Vice President, the Cabinet wives, the entire Diplomatic Corps, the wives of all ninety-six senators, the wives of the 435 Members of Congress, the

Supreme Court and the Chiefs of Staff of the Army, the Navy, and the Marines. All this sounded like a formidable task to me.

As I now read through the stack of letters, I notice long breaks in their sequencing. Whether I was not too communicative at times or whether the letters were too personal and Mama destroyed them, or they were too uninteresting to be preserved, I do not know.

In 1931 we purchased a house in Montgomery. In those days, Lister and I spent about seven months a year in Alabama and five in Washington. The Government was not then engaged in many of the activities that the Great Depression made necessary. Washington was not the hub of the universe as it became after World War II. Before the War, a member of Congress held a very pleasant position. During the Depression his salary was cut to $8,500, which to many of our friends seemed a fortune—but in a city the size of Washington this amount was not adequate. I can recall hearing a certain Congressman say that he had to consider having a pair of pants pressed several times before he spent the money. The expense of a campaign every other year makes the going pretty tough at times.

Following each election year, there was a short session of Congress known as the "lame duck" session because the defeated members were allowed to serve until the month of March following their defeat. That was all changed on February 6, 1933; nowadays, a defeated Congressman goes out in January after the November elections.

During the early days of World War II, I wrote a column each week for the *Birmingham News*. Many of my letters to my mother during this period were copies of the column. In 1956 Mother died and the letters ceased. For a time I forgot about the journal I had been keeping; later, an automobile accident gave me so much leisure time that I began jotting down interesting incidents, which are also included in this manuscript.

Montgomery, Alabama
1974

A Senator's Wife Remembers

Introduction

[The following is the text of a luncheon speech given by Henrietta Hill on February 15th, 1962, at The Elms. According to Mrs. Hill, The Elms "was a French chateau type mansion restored by Mrs. Perle Mesta and was occupied by her for a few years before being sold to Vice President Lyndon Johnson. The Johnsons occupied The Elms until they moved to the White House after President Kennedy's assassination." [Though Mrs. Hill is not specific in her notes, this speech seems to have been given at a Senate Ladies Red Cross luncheon, an organization to which she belonged for many years.]

Not long ago my six-year-old grandson, Clark Hubbard, inquired of his grandfather Hubbard, "Doc, how did you do when the Dinosaurs were here?"

When I was asked to do a bit of reminiscing of the old days when I was new in Washington and Washington was new to me, I felt that somebody was sure to ask me about the Dinosaurs.

I do recall that at the time of my arrival, all native-born Washingtonians were referred to as "Cave Dwellers," and I do remember seeing a Dinosaur in the Museum of Natural History. I hadn't been here very long before I learned to distinguish the female Cave Dwellers from the rest of the population. A female Cave Dweller wore a certain type tall crown black hat, nicknamed a "Dowager Hat." With these Dowager Hats she wore a well-cut black crepe dress, a string of pearls, white gloves and a fur neckpiece. This was elegance supreme.

There were no uncovered heads on the streets of Washington, and no tinted coiffeurs. No lady would think of dyeing her hair. If you suspected one of your friends of this deception, you spoke of it in a whisper (behind her back).

The date of my appearance on the local scene was February 1928. I was a brand new bride just out of school, with a knee length trousseau. My frilly, overdressed wardrobe was clearly labeled "Deep South." At least one person in Washington liked my hats. The fashionable place to dine at this period was the Willard Hotel. Lister and I dined there nearly every Sunday night. In my trousseau was a large black straw John Frederick hat, lined with cream lace. One night when we were dining in the Crystal Room of the Willard, the headwaiter came over, made a deep bow, and said, "Madam, that is the most beautiful hat I have ever seen."

By fall a dreadful calamity befell American women, especially me— overnight, dresses dropped from knee to ankle length. To complicate matters further, my spreading waistline and protruding front had to be covered somehow. I have always envied modern women their pretty maternity clothes. Mine were size 44's cut down in the shoulders and gathered at the waist on elastic. No wonder pregnant women used to sit at home.

My first White House reception was the last Congressional Reception given by the Calvin Coolidges. Mrs. Coolidge was a charming and gracious hostess in spite of a frugal husband. The only refreshment served at this White Tie affair was ice water. As we left the dining room I couldn't help chuckling at a remark the Chief Justice William Howard Taft, made to a lady nearby: "Well, you will have to admit I fed you better when I was President."

Once, Will Rogers spent a night at the White House with the Coolidges. Next day this appeared in his column: "The White House is the only place I was ever served fish for dinner and fish hash for breakfast."

The following year I missed the inauguration of President Hoover by staying in Alabama for the birth of our daughter, Henrietta, in late January. By the time I returned to Washington, for the succeeding session of Congress, the Great Depression was in full swing. Apple vendors and pencil peddlers abounded throughout the city. Congress cut its own salary from ten to eight thousand dollars. Entertaining was cut to a minimum. Everybody gave small dinners at home and played games afterwards for the amusement of the guests. Nobody could afford the theatre or to eat in a restaurant.

The main topic of conversation in the social world was the famous feud over "who outranked whom at the dinner table" between Alice Roosevelt Longworth, wife of the Speaker of the House, and Dolly Gann, the sister of Vice President Charlie Curtis. Big Chief "Rain in the Face" offered this solution: "Tell them to sit in circle Indian fashion, then there be no head no feet."

By spring, the Bonus Army began to march on Washington. I was enlisted by the Red Cross to help feed the hungry men from a rolling canteen. There was a deep, underlying unrest among those men and I have always felt that the American people never fully realized how close we came to a bloody revolution. Franklin Roosevelt brought with him to the Nation's Capital a renewed hope and faith.

I wish I could remember all the political stories I have heard through the past thirty-four years. Here are two of my favorites on the Roosevelts. At night, Franklin praying, "Dear Lord, please make Eleanor just a little bit tired tomorrow." The other is about Eleanor dashing about the country riding on a Pullman car. One night, being unable to sleep because of the loud snoring from the upper, she knocked on the bottom of the berth above, to waken the sleeper. The man above finally leaned over and shouted, "Ah, cut it out. I saw you when you got on."

As the war progressed, living in Washington became exceedingly difficult. We shared our car with neighbors, the Carl Hatches of New Mexico and the Burnett Maybanks of South Carolina. We stood in line at the A&P like the rest of Americans, and I learned to cook, wash and iron, and nurse for the first time in my life—but it wasn't too bad. True, we had blackout curtains hung at our windows at night but no one really feared a bombing. I wish we could feel as secure today.

One good thing came out of the war. Wholesale calling was abandoned and has never been thought necessary since. During my first winter in Washington, Josephine Black, the wife of Alabama's junior Senator, took me with her to make the required calls. This included leaving cards at the White House, on all House members, the members of the Senate, Cabinet, Diplomatic Corps, Chiefs of Staff of the Army and Navy, and all Top Brass. Mondays were the Supreme Court, Tuesdays House, Wednesday Cabinet, Thursdays Senate, Friday for Diplomats, and any day for the White House. Oh, those At Homes! A hostess never knew how many people to expect. Cabinet "At Homes" were a great place to take constituents.

I know you have all had the experience of not hearing a name in an introduction. At first, I used to ask Lister to repeat a name he murmured; after several kicks on the shin, I learned not to ask. The best piece of advice any one ever gave me as a newcomer to Washington was, "Take for granted that no one in Washington knows you and tell them your name."

Most Congressional wives can tell you how they helped elect their husbands to Congress, but not I—I was no help at all. Lister had already been a member of the House for five years when we were married. For the next sixteen years he had no opposition. When he announced his candidacy for the Senate, it coincided with my need to have an operation. The day I returned home from the hospital our house caught fire. The temperature registered twelve degrees, and I caught the flu from the freezing weather. Getting up again for Christmas dinner I slipped and fell, breaking a finger. As I said before, I was no help at all. Folks must have felt sorry for us and felt that Lister needed the job.

PART ONE

1928–1941

Courtship & Early Life

Lister claims I fell in love with him when I heard him make a "Mother's Day" speech at the Kiwanis Club Ladies Night Banquet in Eufaula, Alabama—my hometown—in May 1926. All during dinner, Lister kept flirting with me. My escort for the evening, Arch Roberts, was a bit annoyed.

The Honorable Charles S. McDowell, Lieutenant Governor of Alabama, acted as toastmaster, introducing Lister Hill as the youngest Member of the U.S. House of Representatives (he was first elected in 1923 at the age of twenty-nine) and the most brilliant orator in the state. Lister began his speech by thanking the toastmaster and complimenting the beautiful and charming ladies, and all the mothers. He pulled out all the stops—from Whistler's Mother to the Mother of Ben Hill of Georgia, the U.S. Senator and famous orator. (Ben Hill's mother had plowed the fields to raise the money from a truck garden to educate her son.) Lister ended by quoting, "The hand which rocks the cradle rules the world." There was not a dry eye in the room when he concluded.

It was a year before I saw him again. Lister and several of his cousins were returning from a wedding in Talladega, Alabama. They were all feeling romantic. Elizabeth Hill, one of the passengers, turned to Lister and said, "Why don't you get married?"

"Well," he said, "you find me a girl."

At that time, I would have thought that Lister was more interested in politics than in girls, but Elizabeth had already thought of one. Bright and early the next day she wrote me a note inviting me to come to Montgomery to visit her; she had a surprise for me. Who could resist such an invitation? I went.

I knew nothing of the nature of my "surprise" until Lister walked in.

We dined with the family, and then took off for a movie. I found Lister interesting, but different from the other men I went out with.

In September 1927, my father died. I was in mourning and was not going out socially. Lister was most attentive and sympathetic. We spent many evenings together, sitting before the fire reading *Elbert Hubbard's Scrapbook* and the works of Shakespeare. *Hamlet* is by far Lister's favorite. He reads beautifully—and would have been an actor. One night he picked up a copy of *King Lear*, thumbed through it for a few pages, then paused and read: "'Her voice was ever soft, gentle and low, an excellent thing in woman.' Henrietta, when I heard your voice, that was when I fell in love with you."

By the end of January 1928 we were engaged.

Since Lister was in public life, we had to choose between either a small wedding, or having the ceremony performed in a stadium. Deciding to exchange our vows quietly, we planned to have only our two families and a few friends.

The ceremony was to be performed before the Pier mirror in the parlor of the "Fontaine" home in Columbus, Georgia, on February 20, 1928. The Fontaine house was a white-columned mansion, overlooking the Chattahoochee River, built about 1830. My great-great-grandfather John Maury Fontaine helped build the town of Columbus and served as its first mayor. His granddaughter, Mary Fontaine Pou, was the last member of the family to occupy the Fontaine home.

There is always excitement the day of a wedding. Our cake, a three-tiered, embossed work of art, arrived from Birmingham in pieces. This was barely a challenge to Aunt Mary Pou. She took a large tin pan, turned it bottoms up, then placed an inverted cheese box on top of it; on that she put a cake, purchased from a local bakery. When the three sections were covered with frosting and surrounded with lilies of the valley, it looked like a real bridal cake. The guests were none the wiser—but I am sure they wondered why the bride cut the cake so sparingly.

We had asked Lister's uncle, the Reverend Lot Hill of Athens, Georgia, to perform the ceremony, but an hour before the scheduled time he telephoned us that a train wreck had delayed him beyond hope of his reaching Columbus in time to officiate. The local Episcopal minister, Dr. Alston Wragg, was finally found and pressed into service at the last minute. My sister, Mary Andrews, was my only attendant. Uncle Sam Weyman gave me away, while Lister's father, Dr. L.L. Hill, acted as his son's best man.

As I said before, we had planned a quiet wedding with a simple announcement afterwards—but it didn't work out that way. My initiation into public life commenced with wedding bells and a brass band. A few years before, the leader of the Army Band, Captain William J. Stannard, had promised Congressman Hill he would play at his wedding, in grateful appreciation of a favor.

The favor was as follows: Captain William Stannard had been a Sergeant in the army when he approached Lister one day in the Capitol and asked him for a favor. It seems that all the members of the band outranked him, being lieutenants and captains—and Stannard could not control them. My father agreed to help him and got a bill passed in Congress that awarded the rank of captain to all leaders of military bands.

Now, it was sheer coincidence that the Army Band was on tour at Fort Benning, Georgia (twelve miles from Columbus)—in the right town on the right day. Captain Stannard picked up the local paper on the morning of the wedding and read of the coming event. At eleven o'clock he rang the doorbell of the Fontaine House and announced, "Mr. Hill, I have come to fulfill my promise."

A NOTE ABOUT MY origin: Edwin "Pa" Watson—who became a great friend to FDR—and I were both born in the same town, Eufaula, Alabama. Pa grew up in Virginia, while I stayed on in Alabama, until Lister and I were married. I do not know any of the details of the birth of Pa Watson other than that his grandmother lived in Eufaula, and his mother went home to "Mama" for the birthing. There were few hospitals in the small town throughout the nation; Eufaula had none (though it now has a Hill-Burton Hospital.) An expectant mother depended on family and practical nurses for nursing care.

Pa Watson preceded me by quite a few years. But whatever his beginning it could not have been as dramatic as my introduction to life.

My parents, Etta Copeland and William McCormick, were living in Columbus, Georgia, where I would normally have been born, except that my grandfather, Dr. William Preston Copeland, would deliver my mother of me, and Mama wanted to go home.

The Columbus doctor who attended Mama during her pregnancy advised my father that my arrival could be expected any minute. Papa rushed down to the railroad station and contracted for a private car to be attached to the Central of Georgia train, the "Cannon Ball." A doctor, a nurse, my sister Mary, and my parents boarded the "Cannon Ball," bound for Eufaula, a distance of ninety-eight miles by train, a journey of four or five hours.

My arrival, the doctor had said, could begin any minute—the minutes stretched into hours—the hours into days—the days into weeks. At the end of a month, on December 6, 1904 at eight o'clock in the morning, I put in an appearance.

MARCH 8, 1928
WASHINGTON HOTEL

Lister was staying at the Washington Hotel before we were married, and it is here we planned to live until the end of the year's session of Congress, in early June.

There are several Congressional couples living at the Washington Hotel. Representative and Mrs. Henry Allen Cooper of Wisconsin, Representative and Mrs. Fritz Lanham of Texas, and Representative Jerry Cooper of Tennessee. We all eat in the coffee shop; we can't afford to dine in the main dining room very often.

Mrs. Cooper has been very sweet to me and has given me a lot of helpful advice. I shall try always to remember two things she told me. "My dear, take for granted that no one knows you in Washington, and tell them who you are. Most people are not intentionally rude, but you meet so many people when you are in politics. If they know you that is all to the good; if not, you may have made another friend. It is just as easy to be on time at functions as to be late. Hostesses here wait fifteen minutes for late arrivals. If you are late, it is you who are embarrassed and have to walk in alone." (I bought a map of Washington and studied it.)

Mrs. Cooper entertained today at a luncheon at the Washington Hotel, in honor of Mrs. Peter Golet Gerry of Rhode Island. Mrs. Gerry is president of the "Congressional Club," and was formerly married to George Vanderbilt, the owner of Biltmore Estates, North Carolina. This was my first formal luncheon in Washington. At my place at the table was a card with the picture of a bride, and a bouquet of rosebuds and lilies of the valley tied with a ribbon.

Representative Cooper is the author of a Congressional bill to tear down all the unsightly buildings, hotels, laundries, and other decaying edifices on B Street, Northeast and Northwest, and replace those buildings with Government and District buildings. The new street is to be named "Constitution Avenue."

On Sundays, Lister and I dine in style at the Willard Hotel. The food is better, and we like to get away on our own for a change. Dinner, with all the trimmings, is $1.50.

Not long ago, we were the guests of Ed O'Neil, a charming gentleman who comes from Alabama to lobby for the American Farm Bureau Federation, of which he is president.

After dinner we sat in Peacock Alley to listen to the orchestra play soft music and watch the notables pass by.

MARCH 1928
WASHINGTON HOTEL

The Fritz Lanhams of Texas who live at the Washington gave a small dinner for us last night. After dinner we wandered into an adjoining parlor for a demitasse and conversation. Whenever you gather a group of politicians together, story swapping is sure to begin. On this particular occasion I think Senator Morris Sheppard of Texas told the prize story.

All during his administration, President Coolidge made a practice of inviting Members of Congress for breakfast. The word got around that the cakes and sausage were delicious and the Vermont maple syrup was very special. On the morning that Senator Sheppard was invited to attend one of the White House breakfasts, he rose earlier than usual. It was sunny and bright, with a little nip in the air. The Senator took a deep breath and decided to walk the distance from his home on 19th street to the White House. By the time he reached the Executive Mansion he had worked up a pretty good appetite.

After the guests had all assembled and greetings were exchanged, the butler announced breakfast. Each guest was served a plate with a stack of golden brown cakes and a large sausage. Senator Sheppard had a particular fondness for sausage. Eagerly he picked up his knife and fork and prepared to take a bite when one of Mrs. Coolidge's white wolfhounds came bounding into the room. At this moment President Coolidge told the Senator: "Throw him your sausage."

The Senator reluctantly obeyed, thinking that a butler would be asked to bring him another sausage. But, no—the President buried his face in his plate and kept on eating, saying not another word.

MARCH 20, 1928

The Alabama Society gave a ball last night in honor of Lister and me. We have been married exactly one month. When the invitation to the ball came, I was a bit disturbed. Lister has never been too interested in dancing. I suggested that we go to a nightclub and let me teach him a few new dance steps. He is not exactly a Fred Astaire, but we managed.

MARCH 28, 1928

Yesterday, I took Mrs. William C. Gorgas up to the Capitol with me to hear Lister speak on a bill to set up a Research Laboratory on Tropical Diseases in the Panama Canal Zone, to be known as the "Gorgas Memorial Laboratory." This was the first time I had ever heard Lister make a speech on the floor of the House of Representatives. Imagine how proud I was to hear him speak and to have the bill pass.

[Excerpts from speech about Crawford Gorgas:]

It was in the little town of Toulminville, a suburb of Mobile, Alabama, on the third day of October 1854, William Crawford Gorgas was born. In 1880 yellow fever in its most violent form was exacting a heavy toll of the people of Brownsville, Texas. Gorgas was then a young Lieutenant in the Army Medical Corps. He volunteered to go into the stricken area and was sent to Fort Brown to assist in the medical care of the civilian population.

Gorgas fell victim to the dread disease, and thereby became immune to yellow fever. In 1898 Gorgas was appointed Chief Sanitary Officer at Havana. In 1900 there came to Havana the immortal four: Walter Reed, James Carroll, Jesse W. Lazear, and Aristides Agramonte, the commission charged by the Government of the United States with solving the baffling problem of the cause of yellow fever. The gallant Lazear gave his life by definitely demonstrating that the Stegomyia [yellow fever] mosquito was the infecting agent in yellow fever. In a brief time of seven and one-half months, Gorgas delivered the city from Stegomyia. In 1904 the U.S. Government undertook the stupendous job of digging the Panama Canal, made possible by the eradication of the mosquito. France had tried and failed, as had others, because of health reasons.

When World War One began, Gorgas was appointed Surgeon General of the Army. Gorgas is quoted as saying to the Secretary of War, Newton D. Baker, "I want to give you a fit Army, Mr. Secretary."

Out of this dream of Gorgas, with its vision of a plan to add to the health power of the Nation, has come the Gorgas idea of better personal health through an annual check-up by the family doctor. In his name and honoring his memory and achievements and medical genius has been established the Gorgas Memorial Institute of Preventive and Tropical Medicine—a great organization not only dedicated to added research in tropical medicine, but also pledged to a tremendous educational campaign for better personal health.

April 9, 1928

We entertained at a luncheon last week for Sir St. Clair Thompson. He is a very prominent throat specialist from London, and was house surgeon for Lord Joseph Lister when Dr. Hill (my Lister's father), studied the principals of asepsis and antisepsis under Dr. Lister.

We planned the luncheon at the Willard Hotel and invited Mrs. Gorgas to come. General and Mrs. Gorgas had known Sir St. Clair in England. Since Sir St. Clair was a contemporary of Dr. Hill's, we thought that Mrs. Gorgas was a suitable age for him—but Sir St. Clair had awfully young ideas. He was not the least bit interested in Mrs. Gorgas. After luncheon, Sir St. Clair turned to me and asked, "Mrs. Hill, isn't there some place you and I could go tea dancing this afternoon?"

I sort of gasped and looked in Lister's direction for help. To my utter amazement, Lister replied, "Of course. There is an excellent orchestra at the Mayflower Hotel. I understand they have tea dancing there every afternoon. Henrietta will be delighted to go there with you."

Sir St. Clair was a charming and cultured gentleman. His very British clothes, white hair, and monocle gave him a distinctive look that would attract attention anywhere. He knew all the latest dance steps and tangoed beautifully. I couldn't help feeling a bit conspicuous, as all eyes were focused upon us. Laughing to myself, I thought, "If Dr. Hill could see us now!"

APRIL 1, 1928

Last Friday, March 28, Mrs. Ed Almon invited the wives of the Alabama Congressmen to a luncheon in my honor at the Congress Hall Hotel. There were eight of us, all together. Mrs. Hugo Black from the Senate, Mrs. Miles Allgood, Mrs. John McDuffie, Mrs. William Bowling, Mrs. Will Bankhead, Mrs. George Huddleston, and of course Mrs. Almon and me. (Both Congressman Henry Steagall's wife and Senator "Cotton" Tom Heflin's wife have been dead for some years, and Congressman Buck Oliver has never married.) The ladies have all been very sweet to me and have tried to make me feel welcome. Congressman and Mrs. Almon live at the Congress Hall Hotel on Capitol Hill. After luncheon, Mrs. Almon invited us up to her room for a visit. They presented me with a beautiful after-dinner coffee service. I was simply thrilled, as it was one of the things we needed most. Last week Josephine Black had asked me to go shopping and help pick out a service; she let me pick this one out, thinking it was for her.

The cherry blossoms are in full bloom around the speedway. These are the double pink variety, which bloom about two weeks after the earlier ones around the Tidal Basin. Personally I think the single weeping cherry trees planted around the Basin are far lovelier, and their setting is more artistic. It was a great surprise to learn neither variety bear fruit, nor are they fragrant.

Charles Lindbergh was in town recently and offered to take up any of the Congressmen and their wives who wished to fly with him. He was trying to interest Members of Congress in the future of aviation. I am sorry to say that I had a cold and earache the day he made the offer, and could not go. Someone told me they overheard him say that he was black and blue from the crowds of people who punched him. I suppose they just wanted to say they had touched Lindbergh.

APRIL 20, 1928

On Mondays, I am supposed to call on the wives of the Supreme Court, as that is their official day "At Home" to host afternoon teas. Tuesdays the Congressional wives receive, Wednesdays the Cabinet ladies are "At Home," Thursdays belong to the Senate Ladies, and Friday to the Diplomatic Corps. I haven't gotten it all straight yet.

Mrs. Hugo Black has been kind enough to take me calling with her several times. It is amazing; you ring the doorbell of these official hostesses, most of whom you have never seen, and ask the butler (if they have one), "Is Mrs. Blank receiving today?" Chances are she has left orders that no one is to be admitted that day and you have wasted your time. I am determined to see this calling through, this once—from then on I am only going to call on those who call on me. Everything here is backwards; the newcomers call first.

Most of our invitations are engraved and are sent out at least six weeks before the event takes place. A dinner invitation must be answered within twenty-four hours after it is received and has to be in the form of a formal note. Most formal dinners are at eight o'clock and you have to go in evening clothes—the men wear white ties and tails.

I WISH I HAD someone to help me write my thank-you notes for our wedding presents. Yesterday the Members of the House Military Committee, of which Lister is a member, presented him with a silver tray as a wedding gift. On it are engraved these words: "Presented to the Honorable Lister Hill by the Members of the Committee on Military Affairs, House of Representatives, Congress of the United States, February 20, 1928." The tray goes beautifully with my silver service. The *Montgomery Advertiser* photographer took a picture of the presentation, which appeared in the paper.

THE LAST TWO DAYS every photographer in town has called to take my picture for the Washington papers. This morning I received a call from the *New York Tribune* photographer. If I get a good picture, I will send one to Mama. I don't have a picture taken in my wedding dress. This picture taking is a racket.

APRIL 1928

On Monday, Mrs. William J. Harris, wife of the Senator from Georgia, entertained at a luncheon for me at the Wardman Park Hotel. Mrs. Harris is from Alabama and is the daughter of General Joe Wheeler, whose statue was placed by the state of Alabama in Statuary Hall at the Capitol. Among the other guests at the luncheon were Mrs. Walter George, wife of the Junior Senator from Georgia, Mrs. William Crawford Gorgas, and Mrs. Hugo Black. Mrs. Black is the youngest member of the Alabama delegation, next to me.

SEPTEMBER 1928

Election time is here again. Alabamians were not too enthusiastic over the selection of Alfred E. Smith as the Democratic nominee for the Presidency. Nevertheless, the loyal members of the Democratic Party arranged political rallies throughout the State.

Lister invited me to go with him to Luverne, Alabama, to the first political gathering I had ever attended. I don't recall hearing my mother or father ever discuss politics. Women in the South left politics to the man in the family.

Most of the small towns and rural communities still have clay roads. In summer the highways are dusty, in winter they can be dangerously slick. Cars are old—and few. The South is still suffering from a depression, in spite of the fact that the Republican Presidential nominee, Herbert Hoover, promised a chicken in every pot and declared that prosperity was just around the corner.

Most large gatherings are held in the school auditorium or the courthouse or under the trees. Occasionally there is a barbecue. When we arrived, the auditorium was jam-packed. Latecomers who could not find a seat were sitting in the windows, barring the bit of cool air circulating outside.

The speakers and officials sat on the platform. I found a place near the front door. One by one, the candidates made their bids for the various offices. Lister, the principal speaker of the evening, was last on the list. He began speaking around nine o'clock. After the usual pleasantries, he moved on to the issues of the day: unjust freight rates, "Pittsburgh Plus," mortgage foreclosure, Muscle Shoals, and many more of the South's troubles.

Lister worked his audience into a high pitch. He lifted them out of their seats as he told them the legend of the Earl of Douglas, the mighty Scottish hero who set forth with an army of Crusaders to recover the Holy Grail from the hands of the Turkish infidels. For a time it appeared that the Crusaders were routed and badly defeated, when the Earl of Douglas pitched the heart of Robert Bruce right into the midst of the enemy, crying, "Lead on, oh heart of Bruce! We follow thee. We follow thee." The Crusaders rallied and the battle was won. Then Lister brought forth the "Happy Warrior," the Democratic nominee, Alfred E. Smith.

When the speaking concluded, enthusiastic listeners then made a leap for the platform to shake hands with the young Congressman.

Whether it was the intense heat, the heart of Bruce, or my pregnancy, I don't know, but I felt faint and rushed to the door. A dear little woman with sparkling blue eyes spoke to me. "Can I help you?" she asked, fanning me with a palmetto fan. "I never try to keep up with my husband at one of these gatherings. I just take a seat near the door and when my husband comes through the door, I catch up with him."

On the way home Lister asked, "How did it go?"

"I have married a man with many talents," I said. "You were wonderful."

Lister and I were riding along peacefully. We were both tired. I had been thinking about it all evening and finally I asked, "What is Pittsburgh Plus?"

"Unjust freight rates," he replied. "That is one of the things I think should be abolished immediately if the South is ever to prosper. Pittsburgh Plus means that the South pays the cost of the steel plus the cost of shipping it from Pittsburgh to Birmingham *plus* five dollars a ton."

Lister kept his word and at his first opportunity urged FDR to appoint two Southerners to the Interstate Commerce Commission. (They were J. Haden Alldredge, who served as a member of the ICC from May 1939 until December 1955, and Marion Caskie, who served from August 1935 until April 1940. (Pittsburgh Plus was abolished and the South no longer had to pay unjust freight rates.)

JANUARY 28, 1929

Before the cherry blossoms bloomed again, a new experience came into my life—the most wonderful of all—motherhood. Our daughter, a curly-haired little beauty whom we named Henrietta, was born on January 18, 1929, one month before we were to celebrate our first wedding anniversary. And so it was that Lister went apartment hunting.

Few Congressional families own their own homes. At the end of the session they give up their apartments or rented houses and return home. It is considered very bad policy to own a residence in Washington. Your opponent in a campaign is apt to use it against you, saying, "So he thinks he is a fixture, does he?" As a consequence, most members of Congress have to scurry around and find a place to live at the beginning of each session.

Our first residence, after the birth of our daughter, was at the Fairfax Hotel on Massachusetts Avenue. Here we leased a hotel apartment during the sessions in 1929, 1930, and 1931.

JANUARY 1931
FAIRFAX HOTEL

I have intended to write in my journal for several days but haven't had a minute to sit down at my desk. It seems that I am always in a rush. I have just returned home from driving Lister to the Capitol and doing my marketing and it is now twelve o'clock. My day has just begun and it is already half over. I never get back from the Capitol before eleven o'clock. It takes so much time driving back and forth.

Yesterday afternoon I attended a tea at "Woodley," the home of Mrs. Stimson, the wife of the Secretary of State. They have the most charming house. It is furnished throughout with rare antiques. Recently I heard that Francis Scott Key had once lived at Woodley.

These large Cabinet "At Homes" aren't much fun. You shake hands with the hostess, then wander about the living room into the dining room. Here you are served tea or coffee, cake, and sandwiches. You stand about a bit, then leave. The chances are you didn't know a soul and no one bothered to speak to you, excepting the person you came with. I was talking to Josephine Black the other day and she asked me, "Did you ever notice at a party in Washington, when you are talking to someone and doing your best to be charming, how that person is looking over your head for someone more important to talk to next?"

I hear that lots of Congressmen's wives take their constituents to these "At Homes," as out-of-town people seem to get a great kick out of seeing celebrities. It doesn't seem fair to the hostess to bring uninvited guests. One old lady (I think her name is King) attends most of the "At Homes." She carries a large black pocketbook in which she stuffs sandwiches to carry home. Poor soul—she has become an institution.

The New Deal

HOTEL 2400

Early in the New Deal we took an apartment at the Meridian Mansions at 2400 Sixteenth Street. We had just been settled in our new home a few weeks at the time of Roosevelt's first inauguration. There is one picture that will always be vivid in my mind's eye.

After witnessing the swearing in of Vice President Garner in the Senate Chamber, I started to walk over to the Rotunda to gain access to the main portico where the exercises were to be held. On my way I was stopped by a policeman and asked to stand aside for the President to pass. This was my first glimpse of Franklin Roosevelt, the President-elect. He was leaning on the arm of his son James. I had not realized until then what a tremendous effort it was for him to manipulate his crippled legs. It gave me a feeling of his greatness that he could conquer such a physical handicap. Never have I seen such an expression as he wore on his face—it was faith, it was courage, it was complete exultation!

The day after the Inauguration came the shock of the Bank Holiday. Many people from around the country had come for the Inauguration and found themselves without funds to return home. We had invited guests for dinner that night: Mrs. Henry D. Clayton, the wife of a Federal Judge of Alabama, and her two nieces, Lillian and Betty Rossell. They too were suffering from the enforced Bank Holiday and were without cash and most grateful for a free meal.

In the early days of the New Deal, many interesting people were brought to Washington—professors, economists, bankers, lawyers, and some of the best brains in the country. President Roosevelt was searching

34

for new ideas to pull Americans out of the deep financial depression. It was an exciting time. Lister and I heard many ideas advanced, many of which are now permanent laws.

Two of our favorite New Dealers were Lucy and Jonathan Daniels. Jonathan, the son of Ambassador Josephus Daniels, came to Washington as an assistant to Franklin Roosevelt.

The fact that Franklin Roosevelt and the New Deal were able to meet the needs of the people with a bloodless revolution has always been to me one of the greatest achievements in American history. I am proud that Lister and I could have had a small part in this stupendous drama.

THE FOLLOWING STORY WAS told by Josh Lee, the Senator from Oklahoma, during a party at our house:

In the early days of the Great Depression, poverty and dust covered most of the midwestern states, which surrounded the dust bowl. Oklahoma was virtually bankrupt.

Old Uncle Billy, a farmer, rode into town once a week to purchase the few meager supplies he could afford to buy. As he chugged along in his Model T Ford, he heard an explosion, then another. When a sweating, swearing Uncle Billy climbed out of his jalopy to take a look at the tires, the other two tires went down. Rusty boiling water gushed from the radiator.

Uncle Billy looked around for help. He had parked alongside the State Mental Institute. The grass was pretty and green, the garden well tended, and there were nurses in white running around waiting on the patients.

An old man peering through an iron gate surrounding the enclosure began a conversation with Uncle Billy. "Hidy," he said.

Uncle Billy replied, "Good morning." Uncle Billy looked longingly at the benches under the trees. "Looks like you have a nice place there. How is the cooking?"

"Fine, just fine," replied the inmate. "We don't have nothing to do except sit around in the sunshine." The old man paused for a moment, then asked, "Have you ever been crazy?"

Uncle Billy shook his head. "Nope, nope, I haven't ever been crazy."

The inmate looked squarely at Uncle Billy and said, "It beats farming."

JANUARY 3, 1934

Shortly after the New Year's Holidays, Lister, Henrietta, and I returned to Washington on the *Crescent Limited*. Among the passengers on the train was an elderly woman all dressed in black. She had a rather large frame. Her complexion was sallow and wrinkled. Before we reached our destination Lister engaged in conversation with her. To his surprise he found that she was Mrs. Edward Fitzgerald, mother of F. Scott Fitzgerald. Mrs. Fitzgerald had been down to Alabama to spend the Christmas Holidays with Scott, his wife Zelda, and their daughter Scottie. The young Fitzgeralds have rented a house for the winter in Montgomery, Alabama, Zelda's hometown.

When we arrived in Washington, Lister and I offered to share a taxi with Mrs. Fitzgerald. We asked for her address and found that we were all bound for the same destination—Meridian Mansions, 2400 Sixteenth Street, N.W.

As time went by, we became increasingly fond of Mrs. Fitzgerald. She was a lonely soul. I frequently took her to ride with Henrietta and me in Rock Creek Park or to Hains Point.

Last Wednesday, Mrs. Fitzgerald handed me a recent copy of the *Saturday Evening Post*. "There is an article in here by Scott. I want you to read it and tell me what you think."

I took the *Post* and promised to telephone her as soon as I had time to read it. By the time I had finished her son's narrative, I understood why she was concerned. This was clearly not up to Scott's usual high standard. Later on that day, when I reported to Mrs. Fitzgerald, she immediately sensed that we were in agreement. I tried to gloss it over, but there was no use. The old lady was clearly disturbed.

TUESDAY, FEBRUARY 24, 1933
2400 SIXTEENTH STREET, N.W.

Last night we gave a dinner in honor of General Douglas MacArthur, who is Chief of Staff of the Army. It was my first large formal dinner. Early in the evening it began to snow and by seven o'clock there were four or five inches of snow on the ground. As a consequence, a number of people dropped out at the last minute. Among those who telephoned to say they could not get there was the Assistant Secretary of State Walton Moore, who lives in Fairfax, Virginia. I can't say I blame him. Fairfax is about fifteen miles from Washington.

Every time anyone dropped out I had to reseat the dinner. At the last minute, I went down to the private dining room to put place cards on the table. I was busy reseating the guests for the fourth time when in walked Mrs. Fitzgerald. She wanted to see the table. When she looked at Mrs. Huse's placecard she remarked, "Have you ever noticed the way Mrs. Huse greets people with great formality during the social season and how much more informal and relaxed she is when the social season is over?" Mrs. Fitzgerald is a dear old soul and I am very fond of her, but she talked so much that she got me all confused and I seated everyone who should have sat on my right, on my left.

It wasn't until everyone sat that I realized my mistake. All evening the guests kept whispering to each other and wondering why I let the Chief of Staff outrank a Senator.

To make matters worse, General MacArthur was the most difficult person to talk to that I have ever run across. After trying several subjects, I asked in desperation, "General, did you fight in the World War?" The General coughed and sputtered, then gulped, then turned to the lady on his right and never addressed another remark to me. I knew better, but I will say, in my defense, I was still in sox and pigtails when the war ended. I wonder if I will ever live it down.

SOME WEEKS AFTER THE inauguration, Zelda Fitzgerald came for a visit. It was the first time I had ever met her. She was still a beautiful woman.

Since we both had Montgomery backgrounds, we had a lot of mutual friends in Alabama. That night, Mrs. Fitzgerald took us to see Tallulah Bankhead in *The Little Foxes*. We all enjoyed it tremendously. I think it was the best play Tallulah ever starred in.

Around Easter-time, Scottie Fitzgerald arrived for a visit to her grandmother. She was then about twelve years old. Mrs. Fitzgerald did not feel equal to taking Scottie sightseeing, so I volunteered. She was a darling little girl, filled to the brim with enthusiasm. We took the usual tourist tour of the Capitol City, the White House, Washington Monument, Library of Congress, Capitol, and the Supreme Court. Surprisingly, the Supreme Court seemed to stimulate her interest most. Her grandfather, Judge A.D. Sayre of Montgomery, served many years on the Circuit Court there. Later he became a Judge on the Alabama Supreme Court.

At the stroke of twelve, the Marshall of the Supreme Court entered the Chamber and in an impressive manner intoned, "Ayez, ayez, ayez. All persons having business before this Honorable, the Supreme Court of the United States, are admonished to draw near and give their attention, for the Court is now in session. God save the United States and this Honorable Court."

Scottie kept punching me. "Where is the accused? Where is the accused?" The Marshall looked angrily at the two of us. "Sh! Sh!" I said, "I will tell you later."

April 6, 1933

Last week I attended a tea at Admiral and Mrs. Mark Bristol's, given for a Baroness Wrangle. The Bristols come from Mobile.

They are a very popular couple and are invited everywhere. Some days they attend as many as four or five parties in an afternoon. I had to laugh at a remark Virginia Blakely (wife of Admiral Charles B.) made about the Bristols. "They are so busy getting to the next party they can't enjoy the party they are at." Mrs. Bristol wears an interesting medal, a large crescent with jewels, which was given to her by the Sultan of Turkey for the outstanding Red Cross work she did after the last war. The Admiral was stationed there at the time and was Acting Ambassador.

I met a Russian woman at the Bristol's party (she is a White Russian—a non-communist—as opposed to a Red Russian) who invited me to a party for a Russian princess next afternoon. The Russians are quite attractive, but I do not like their food. They put sour cream on soup, on caviar, and on a lot of other dishes.

MAY 1933

Early one morning this month, Mrs. Fitzgerald telephoned me. She was very agitated. She had to get to Baltimore to see Scott immediately on urgent business. Could I possibly drive her over? Baltimore is fifty miles from Washington, and I had many things on hand to attend to on a Monday morning. Because she was eighty years old and a lady in great distress, I agreed to drive her over.

It was my intention to call a friend in Baltimore and take her to lunch, but Mrs. Fitzgerald insisted that Zelda was expecting me to be her guest for luncheon. Mrs. Fitzgerald was afraid that if I left her I might get lost trying to find Scott's house again. Their rented home—a Victorian wood-frame structure—was about ten or twelve miles from the heart of Baltimore. I stopped the car, helped Mrs. Fitzgerald out, then sat back in the car.

"I will only be a minute," she said. Finally, she reappeared. "Come on in," she called. It was evident that she had gone in to case the situation. Zelda couldn't have been more gracious.

Eventually, Scott emerged. I wished that I'd had a movie camera with me. When Scott was introduced, he bowed to the floor in a deep cavalier's sweep. It was all I could do to keep from laughing. It was a ridiculous performance—but I understood his annoyance—a strange lady invading their privacy on a Monday morning (possibly the Day After a long, liquid Night Before). As we entered the dining room Zelda rebuked the author, "Oh, Scott, cut it out."

JUNE 1933

We are giving up our apartment at 2400 when we go home to Alabama tomorrow. We can't afford to keep it on a yearly basis. Our lease reads "For the duration of the present session of Congress." The cut from $10,000 to $8000 does not allow many luxuries. Next session we will be looking for another place for our family to live. I have been packing for three days. The silver and all the odds and ends go in the car with Lister to Alabama; the china and linens to the office. Winter clothes are shipped by express.

When Mrs. Fitzgerald heard we were leaving for home, she asked if she could take Henrietta and me to the station to see us off. I insisted that she not take the trouble, but she was very insistent because, said she, "It is so sad to go away and have no one to wave goodbye to you—or welcome you when you return."

We never saw her again.

JANUARY 1934

We have just received our first invitation to a White House dinner on Tuesday, January 23, 1934. I am all excited and have already written a note of acceptance to the Chief of Protocol. We have been to several large receptions, but this is the first time we have been invited to a dinner

General and Mrs. Benjamin Foulois invited us to a dinner on the 22nd. (I am being invited to quite a few things.) The Foulois' dinner was held at the Shoreham Hotel. It was one of the largest parties I have attended. As Lister and I were leaving, we overheard Senator James Hamilton Lewis of Illinois remark to his wife, "My dear, mighty like a barbecue, mighty like a barbecue."

Senator Lewis and his wife, Rose Lawton Douglass, are two of the most colorful characters in Washington. He covers his baldness with a red toupé, but grows his own chin whiskers. When he enters the Senate Chamber, the Illinois Senator looks "very grand" dressed in a morning suit with a cream colored vest and *pince nez* glasses attached to a black ribbon worn around his neck.

Senator Lewis has courtly manners, has never lost his Southern accent, and is known as a silver-tongued orator. There are many legends about him. In 1930, Ruth Hannah McCormick tried to unseat the veteran Senator. Senator Lewis campaigned vigorously but he never referred to his opponent except as "the charming little lady," and he eventually won by a handsome majority.

During one of his campaigns, a friend visited Senator Lewis and advised him to go home and change into something less formal. "You are going into a rather rough neighborhood in Chicago." Senator Lewis went home, changed into a full dress suit, doffed a silk hat, threw an opera cape around his shoulders, carried a gold-headed cane, and away he went. When he reached the hall in which he was to speak, he walked out onto the stage and began, "My friends, I have been warned not to address you here tonight, wearing my best clothes, but, my friends, you deserve the best." The applause was deafening. Lewis carried every box in the beat.

Few persons knew Mrs. Lewis as Rose. Somewhere along the line she was called "Gypsy." She is an expert palmist, and has told many a fortune at church bazaars. Her predictions are uncannily accurate. Mrs. Lewis tells this story on herself: One day she was gazing in a shop window looking at lingerie when a strange woman walked up to her and said, "Pretty, ain't they?" Mrs. Lewis turned around and said, "Could you possibly be addressing me?" The stranger replied angrily, "You need not be so huffy with me. I've seen you running around with that old Senator Lewis."

Gypsy has no sense of time; friends have learned to invite her an hour before their other guests are expected to arrive.

I took Margaret Hamilton to the Japanese Embassy yesterday to a tea. The Ambassador's wife is really very attractive, and the Embassy is the most artistic in Washington. In the entrance hall are several antique suits of armor. The living room is done in a pale yellow and the carpet on the floor is a soft pea green. All around are lovely screens and Japanese prints. It is really like taking a trip to another land. So few of the Embassies feature their native furnishings, which I think is a mistake. Most Americans are looking for the exotic and unusual in foreign embassies. Many of the embassies were bought from rich Americans and are furnished throughout with the former owner's belongings.

Lister had an engagement for dinner with Mike Denny, President of the University of Alabama, so I made Margaret and Claude Hamilton stay for supper with me. After supper we went to a movie called *As Husbands Go.*

I have decided to affiliate with the Washington Junior League when I am in town. It is the only way I can make the required hours for membership each month. This morning I attended one of their meetings and have signed up for work with the marionette group. I worked with puppets for several years in the Montgomery League. Marionettes are much more difficult to manage but they can do more than puppets. I was awfully glad to meet a few young people who are nearer my age. Most of the wives of Members of Congress are so much older than I am. I get pretty lonely at times for someone my own age.

JANUARY 24, 1934

Last night's White House dinner was quite an occasion. The President and Mrs. Roosevelt had as their house guests the famous scientist Professor Einstein and his wife. The Professor wears a shaggy beard and has sort of a remote look, as if he were barely on this earth. Maybe he can escape into the fourth dimension—that might be a pleasant interlude on certain occasions.

After dinner, the gentleman remained in the dining room for coffee and cigars while the ladies retired to the Green Room. I had quite a long conversation with Mrs. Curtis Dall, the President's daughter. She was friendly and attractive and I enjoyed meeting her.

My dinner partners, Representative Tom of Ohio and Governor Herman Kump of West Virginia, were both very attractive men. Among the other guests at the dinner were the Henry Morganthaus, Sr. (parents of the Secretary of the Treasury), Dr. and Mrs. Rex Tugwell, the David Lawrences (editor of the *United States Daily*), and Mr. and Mrs. Averell Harriman of New York (he is part owner of *Time* Magazine and a very handsome man), Senator and Mrs. Henry W. Keyes (Francis Parkinson Keyes, the author), Senator and Mrs. Walter George, Miss Margaret Leland (FDR's secretary).

Two hundred additional guests were invited for the musicals that followed. The program last evening was an all-Indian program with Princess Atalie and Chief Yowlachie singing, in Indian regalia. The loveliest thing they sang was a song called "By the Weeping Waters," a Sioux song by Lieurance. Mrs. Roosevelt seems to feature Americana in her selections of performers at the White House.

APRIL 1934

This morning I took Dell (Henrietta's nurse) and Henrietta to the White House Easter Egg Rolling, which is held every Easter Monday on the White House lawn. I wasn't a bit anxious for Henrietta to go since I could not stay with them, but Dell was wild to see the White House. Dell packed a lunch and Henrietta took her little Easter basket of eggs along and I drove them to the White House and left them at the gate. I had a dental appointment and promised to return for them in about two hours.

The White House gates open as early as eight o'clock in the morning. Children of all ages and races arrive with their baskets of bright colored Easter eggs swung on their arms, accompanied by their parents, or nurses, carrying lunch boxes.

On this occasion no adults are admitted to the White House grounds unless they bring a child with them. Many spinsters or childless matrons who wish to join in the festivities hire a child, for the sum of ten cents, from the band of young racketeers who stand at the entrance and clamor for a "Mama." As soon as the customers are inside the gates of the White House, the young rascals scoot out of a different gate to look for new prospective "Mamas."

Red Cross tents dot the lawn, prepared to administer first aid to all minor injuries, while an ambulance waits outside in case of a serious mishap. The Girl Scouts and Boy Scouts are on hand to guide and direct the crowd, and to play with the children. The Marine Band, in bright red uniforms, plays on the lawn, adding the right touch of gaiety to the festivities.

By mid-afternoon it is difficult to find standing room so great are the crowds. The afternoon paper estimated today's egg rollers to number eight thousand children. The highlight of the occasion was the appearance of the President and Mrs. Roosevelt on the South Portico. I returned to pick up Henrietta and Dell just about the time the Roosevelts appeared. Such cheering, such a welcome they received!

It took me about thirty minutes to locate Dell and Henrietta. When I found them, Dell was weeping copiously. "Lordy, am I glad to see you, Miss Henrietta." It took me some minutes to find out the trouble. Dell had sat down on the lawn under a tree to rest. A group of Girl Scouts, seeing Henrietta playing alone, asked if she might join a game with them, promising to take good care of her. As the crowds grew thicker, Dell could not find her little charge. Eventually she located a policeman who took her to the Lost and Found tent, and there sitting with a sucker in her mouth sat our child.

It will take an army to clean up the White House lawn. There were paper and eggshells and every known kind of debris scattered about. With it all, however, will be the memory of such fun!

MAY 1934

I have just finished writing my acceptance to Mrs. Roosevelt, regarding a luncheon at the White House next Tuesday. I had a previous engagement, but it is more or less unwritten law here than an invitation to the White House must be accepted unless illness or absence prevents. I am curious to know whom she is entertaining.

Today, I had luncheon at the Mayflower Hotel with Grace Snow, daughter of Senator Overman of North Carolina. After lunch we ran into Mrs. Jack Bell of Texas whom we both know rather well. Mrs. Bell was accompanied by the artist Chandor and his wife. Chandor is an Englishman; his wife is a Texan. At present he is painting a portrait of President Roosevelt, which is to be hung in the White House. Strange to say, it depicts FDR in a full length, standing position. I suppose the President does not wish to be remembered as a cripple. (It might be of interest to know that years later an anonymous donor purchased Chandor's portrait of Mrs. Roosevelt and presented it to the White House. It hangs in the hall near the entrance to the East Room. Chandor's portrait is one of the two portraits for which Mrs. Roosevelt posed. The other one is said to belong to her son Elliott.)

Virginia Lyons Blakely took me to the Society of Sponsors luncheon yesterday at the Mayflower. The Sponsors organization is a group of women who have all christened combatant ships. Virginia christened a submarine, the "Blakely." Mrs. Roosevelt was at the luncheon and gave a word of greeting.

Lister has gone to the prizefight tonight. I could not be paid to go to one.

Governor and Mrs. Graves are supposed to come back to Washington next week. The Alabama Society (a delegation of Senators and Congressmen) plans to give a dinner dance in their honor. We expect to attend.

I had a group of girls from Randolph Macon College for lunch on Friday. After lunch I took them sightseeing. There is nothing more wearing than sightseeing. I bet I have been in the Washington Monument a dozen times this spring.

KATE AND COMER JENNINGS (of Eufaula, Alabama) came to supper last night with Donald Comer and Congressman Henry Steagall. I had not known Donald before; he is lovely. I am sorry that Kate is leaving for home tonight. I have enjoyed seeing her and hate to have her go. Comer, who has been here in an advisory capacity with the NRA, will leave soon.

Mr. Steagall, who is Chairman of the House Banking and Currency Committee, was most interesting. He spent the evening discussing a bill that he has introduced in Congress, in which the Government guarantees bank deposits up to five thousand dollars. He thinks this should put a stop to runs on banks and bank failures in the future.

Lawrence Tibbett is to sing at a ceremony at the Capitol on Sunday to commemorate the one hundredth anniversary of the death of General Lafayette. Roosevelt will make the address. I do hope that we will be able to go.

FEBRUARY 16, 1935

Mrs. Jim LeCron (Mrs. LeCron is a sister of Mike and John Cowles, owners of Cowles Publications, which publishes *Look* magazine), whose husband is an assistant to Henry Wallace, entertained at a small luncheon today for Mrs. Wallace. There were only eight guests and they were all very nice. Mrs. Wallace is the best looking [wife of a] member of the Cabinet. When she first came to town she wore heavy horn-rimmed glasses and was not too stylish looking, but somebody took her in tow and now she is exceedingly well dressed. Unless I miss my guess, Secretary Wallace will run for President next time.

FEBRUARY 1935

Lister has told the story of Billy Mitchell so often that I think I know it backwards and forwards. Billy Mitchell underwent court martial and was censored for his then-radical views on air power. Billy felt that the Government should recognize the importance of planes for combat duty. There were a few men in the Air Corps who agreed with him—Colonel Walter Weaver, whom we had known at Maxwell Air Force Base in Montgomery; General James Fechet, Chief of Air Corps; and General Foulois, who later became Chief of Air Corps—and Lister.

Billy Mitchell went to Lister's office in the House of Representatives one morning to talk on his favorite subject, the importance of air combat. Lister finally had to tell the Colonel that he had a White House appointment and had to leave. The Colonel offered to drive Lister to the White House, where he left him at the gate.

Franklin Roosevelt received Lister in his private office. Lister was waiting for him, loaded with Billy Mitchell's arguments on air power. Perhaps Lister was a bit too enthusiastic, so much so that FDR reached over and grabbed his arm. "Lister, my boy," he said. "You have forgotten one thing. We have two best friends in the world, the Atlantic Ocean on one side of us, and the Pacific Ocean on the other side."

Forty-eight hours after Billy Mitchell put Lister out at the gate of the White House, he was dead of a heart attack. His posthumous award, some years later, was of small comfort.

February 15, 1936
1618 Gilmer
Montgomery, Alabama

Our newly arrived young son began life with this headline in the *Montgomery Advertiser*: "Congressman wins race with Stork by a Lash"

Lister had planned to be on hand for the birth of his child, but his son and heir grew impatient and put in an appearance ahead of time. We named our new baby Luther Lister Hill, a combination of his father's and grandfather's names.

Because of the birth of our son, the children and I did not return to Washington in 1936. In the summer of 1931 we had purchased a small clapboard house in Montgomery, Alabama. It is a charming little house. This was our first spring in our own home. Flowers were rampant. Down the driveway, the hollyhocks, larkspurs, and poppies grow in profusion.

We missed Lister, but he was able to visit us often. My mother (Etta McCormick Dent), sister Mary McCormick Andrews, and all of Lister's family were there to help out if we needed them.

Touring the Battle Monuments

Our trip back to Washington was not too bad. Belle Murphy accompanied us on the train to help with the children.

The apartment Lister has rented for us during the 1937 session of Congress only has two bedrooms and a bath. It is bright and sunny, has a few good antiques, and is really very nice and quite attractive. It is far from elegant, but better than the average furnished apartment. I have seen some dreadful ones. Entertaining will have to be at a minimum with just a few people at a time, and very informal. We all long for the little house in Alabama.

I haven't done anything all day except unpack. Our closet space is a bit limited, but we can make out some way. The cook we had last year telephoned Lister to ask if I was in town, and if I would need her. Unfortunately, I have lost her address. I am hoping she will call again.

Tomorrow is the White House dinner. I have a date this afternoon to have my hair done.

The weather is quite warm, for Washington, at this time of the year.

I have made the most wonderful discovery since coming back to D.C. You can now rent diapers from a concern known as the Didee Wash. With Pablum for cereal instead of cooked cereal and no diapers to wash I am now emancipated. I understand that two young men who sat in the park here, trying to figure out some way to make a living, noticed how a mother changed a baby in an afternoon and decided to go into the Baby Laundry business. They will make a fortune. My doctor says it is perfectly safe.

48

INAUGURATION DAY – JAN. 20, 1937

We are all pretty well worn out after the Inauguration. It began raining last night and is still raining. This was one of the worst days I have ever known. It poured all day, and was cold and penetrated to your very bones.

Henrietta and I were fortunate. Having an official tag we were able to drive right to the Capitol door, while the majority of people had to walk for blocks in the pouring rain. Our seats were on the main portico, not far from the place where the President took the oath of office. Had we not been under cover, I don't believe I would have stood for hours as thousands did, in that downpour. Immediately after the President's speech, we met Lister in the House Restaurant where we had luncheon. Then we went to Mr. Steagall's office in the House Office Building, got ourselves an easy chair and watched the parade. I certainly felt sorry for the West Point Cadets who stood in line right outside the window. I was told that both the Cadets and the Naval Midshipmen had to stand in formation for six hours preceding the parade.

The President, not wishing to disappoint the crowd, had the top of his car lowered, and rode bareheaded back to the White House, so all the drenched spectators might be rewarded with a view of their President.

Governor Graves of Alabama brought thirty-five members of his staff to the Inauguration. They all seemed to have a wonderful time. The Alabama Delegation entertained for them at a luncheon while they were here. I sat between the Governor and William Baldwin from Montgomery.

JOSEPHINE BLACK IS ENTERTAINING the ladies of the Governor's staff, who have come for the Inauguration, at a buffet luncheon tomorrow. We took a crowd to the Shoreham Hotel for dinner Monday night, which was all we could do since I have no maid.

The White House dinner last night was given in honor of the Speaker of the House and Mrs. Bankhead. The Hugo Blacks, Mr. Steagall, Lister, and myself were the only other Alabamians present. I think there were seventy-five total guests there.

Mrs. Roosevelt wore a white evening gown that is very much like my brocade except that it had a lace drapery from the shoulder.

The table was set with the Dolly Madison Gold Service; even the flatware—knives, forks, and spoon—were gold. After dinner there was a musical in the East Room. Additional guests were invited for this.

JANUARY 29, 1937
2311 CONNECTICUT AVE.

This is the first real winter day we have had. Up until now it has been very warm, with no snow. It isn't snowing now though it looks a bit threatening and is bitter cold.

On Friday of last week, Colonel George Patton, who is the Commanding Officer at Ft. Meyer, Virginia, entertained for the House Military Committee at luncheon in his quarters. In the afternoon, following the luncheon, there was a horseshow in honor of Lister, who is the Chairman of the Military Committee.

Ft. Meyer is a cavalry post and boasts some of the finest horses and horsemen in the country. Their shows are always spectacular and colorful with the flags flying and the band playing.

After the show was over, there was a tea at the Officers Club. Lister and I stood in the receiving line and were introduced to the officers and their wives.

Several days ago we attended a party that Colonel and Mrs. Edwin Watson gave in honor of Mrs. Hugh Gibson, wife of our Ambassador to Belgium. Mrs. Watson, who is known professionally by her maiden name as Frances Nash, is a concert pianist. I heard her play one night after dinner at the French Embassy. Her music was magical and the piano literally sang. I sat entranced. I understand she practices six hours a day.

Colonel "Pa" Watson is a tall, strong, heavy-set man with a genial personality. It is no wonder the President has chosen him as his personal aide. Whenever the President goes out, he is almost always holding on to Colonel Watson's arm. While Mrs. Roosevelt is out attending the many Birthday Balls, the President celebrates his birthday by entertaining a few of his close friends at the White House with a card game. Three of his special favorites are Pat Watson, Marvin McIntyre, and Admiral Grayson.

Mrs. James Roosevelt, Jr., came to call on me this afternoon. Jimmie is to act as one of his father's secretaries; they have just moved to Washington. I hear that the President is particularly fond of Betsy and that she will fill in for Mrs. Roosevelt when she is out of town, as she frequently is.

FEBRUARY 1937
2311 CONNECTICUT AVENUE

It has snowed, without ceasing, for the past forty-eight hours. I am glad that Henrietta is having Spring Vacation, and that I do not have to go out in this weather.

Last Thursday I attended a luncheon given by the wife of an Attaché at the British Embassy. She is sailing in two weeks for the Coronation of King George. On her piano sat an autographed photograph of the Duke of Windsor. My hostess said that she was not as enthusiastic as she would be if it were Edward. Most of the English people seem to feel that way. Edward had visited them in the Argentine. They found him a very shy man who had always preferred American women.

APRIL 6, 1937

Lister and I had a very pleasant time in New York. I was glad to see the city again as I had not been there in twelve years. It was a tiresome trip, and we would have had a more enjoyable time if we could have been on a holiday and done more of the things we wanted to do. We left here Friday afternoon and reached New York in time for dinner and to see a play. The play we went to see was called *Wingless Victory* by Maxwell Anderson. Katherine Cornell, who took the leading part, did a magnificent job of acting. It was a powerful but morbid story about a sailor who married a Malay princess and tried to bring her home to Salem, Massachusetts, to live.

Saturday morning we went sightseeing, then had lunch. In the afternoon we viewed the Army Day Parade on Fifth Avenue. I wore my fur coat and was wrapped up in two blankets but still nearly froze to death with that icy wind blowing off the river. The parade lasted nearly three hours while twenty-five thousand people passed in review, including former presidential candidate Al Smith and DNC Chairman Jim Farley.

We sat in the reviewing stand with Governor and Mrs. Lehman of New York. Since Lister is Chairman of the House Military Committee, he stood with the Governor and took salutes for three hours. Later there was a banquet; Lister was the principal speaker. The speech was broadcast.

I can't say the trip was too much fun, but it was a change just to get away from home.

APRIL 14, 1937

Yesterday I attended a very swank wedding. The bride is the daughter of Ruth Hanna McCormick, a former Congresswoman of Chicago. Lister would not go, but I went out of curiosity to see the house, which is one of the oldest and finest in Georgetown.

The bride carried a Prayer Book with a shower of pansy orchids. The bridesmaids' dresses were pink with long pink capes of satin and chiffon. They carried pink Gerbera daisies. Little Paulina Longworth, the daughter of Alice Roosevelt Longworth, was the flower girl.

The reception, which was held in the garden of the house in Georgetown, was very gay with an orchestra playing all afternoon. Liveried butlers passed champagne on silver trays throughout the reception. The only person there I knew was a Congressman's wife from Virginia, Mary Bland. We found a seat under the trees and sat there viewing the crowd and had a very, very pleasant time.

APRIL 1937

We have just returned this morning from a boat trip to Williamsburg, Yorktown, and Newport News. The Vice President, Jack Garner of Texas, Senator and Mrs. Joe Robinson of Arkansas, Senator Harry Byrd of Virginia, and a number of other Senators and Congressmen and their wives were on board. The Virginia Historical Society gave the trip to us. We were royally entertained.

I had not seen Williamsburg in some years and I was so interested to see how the restorations had progressed.

The weather was simply dreadful. Coming back, we ran into a storm just outside the Old Point Comfort. We were seated at a table with Leslie Biffle when the boat began to rock, dishes slid off the table. I jumped up and started to run out of the dining room. Les followed me, and as we reached the top of the stairs, he asked, "Where do you want to go, to your room or to the rail?"

"Neither," I replied, "Look behind you." I have never seen such chaos: dishes, tables, chairs, and people all mixed up together. There were screams in all directions. I heard afterwards that Mrs. O'Mahoney of Wyoming and Mrs. Gillett of Iowa had broken arms and legs. The storm raged all night. Lister and I went to our stateroom and lay on the bed. You couldn't walk for fear of falling. Both of us were deathly ill all night. When we arrived back in Washington after the night of horror we found that the water was over the docks and we would probably have to go ashore in small boats. This did not prove to be true. Next time I will go by land.

I poured tea for Mrs. Harry Woodring, the wife of the Secretary of War, at Woodlawn last Thursday. Mrs. Oscar Underwood of Alabama owns Woodlawn but has leased it to the Woodrings for the winter. It was built by George Washington, the foster father of Eleanor "Nelly" Custis, and is considered the finest example of late Georgian architecture in America. The architect, William Thornton, was also the architect for the U.S. Capitol.

MAY 1937

Tuesday night we had dinner with Mr. Frederick A. Delano, the uncle of the President. Mr. Delano's wife is dead, so his daughter-in-law, Mrs. Preston Delano, acts as his hostess when he entertains. Our host lives at 2400 Sixteenth Street, where we used to have an apartment. His apartment is beautifully furnished. He is quite an art connoisseur.

The dinner was given for the Chairman of the Board of TVA, Dr. A.E. Morgan and Mrs. Morgan, who were Mr. Delano's houseguests. The only other guests were the Dean of the Harvard Law School, Jim Landis and Mrs. Landis, and the Hills.

The menu began with a hot broiled grapefruit with rum poured over it, then consommé, a creamed lobster course, leg of lamb with vegetables, a salad, and ice cream and cake.

Dr. Morgan and Lister spent the evening talking over the problems of the Tennessee Valley Authority. I have lived with discussions on Muscle Shoals and TVA ever since Lister and I were married; in fact TVA has almost become a personality to me. The power from TVA has been a wonderful thing industrially for Alabama. Now with the REA (Rural Electrical Association) Co-ops, the farmers have a new way of life open to them. It was very interesting to hear Dr. Morgan tell of the marvelous developments of that entire area.

Before the evening was over, we all talked about Senator George Norris, the father of TVA. Lister is the co-author of the Tennessee Valley Authority, but it was George Norris who conceived the idea of using Muscle Shoals to generate cheap electric power for the farmers of the South.

Some years ago, Senator and Mrs. Norris took a motor trip through Canada. While on this trip they visited a number of isolated farmhouses and were surprised to find electricity in the poorest of the houses. They were delighted to learn that Canada had Government operation of electric power and a well-organized rural electrification association. It was then that George Norris began to dream of carrying electricity to the famers of the United States.

For years he fought a lone and bitter battle in the Senate. In spite of the opposition to his plan, he was revered by all for his honesty, his integrity, and his consistency. Today he is known as the Grand Old Man of the Senate.

Senator Norris can now point with pride to Alabama's TVA and rural electrification—the beginning of a dream come true. As the Senator so rightly said in conversation recently, "Where would American be today without TVA for National Defense?"

Sunday, June 23, 1937

Yesterday we went to a party that the Dick Wilmers gave. Dick is the son of the famous Dr. Richard Wilmer and a grandson of the Bishop.

His wife was Margaret Grant of Atlanta, and a sister-in-law of Josephine Connors of Birmingham.

The Wilmers have a wonderful portrait of the old Bishop. During luncheon, Dick told me an amusing story on his grandfather. It seems that one day one of his parishioners asked, "Bishop, do you approve of smoking?"

"Oh no," replied the Bishop.

"Do you approve of drinking?"

"No, no," said he shaking his head.

"Do you approve of dancing?"

"Absolutely no." Then the Bishop added in a gay mood, "But why let the sinners have all the fun?"

JUNE 1937

Lister's sister, Lillian Hill Rucker, who has been our recent houseguest, has departed. We had a very gay time while she was here. Sunday we took a lovely drive over the new Skyline Drive. It is built on the crest of the Blue Ridge Mountains. You can see almost all of the Shenandoah Valley from there. It is a glorious sight. The mountain laurel was in full bloom and grew in profusion all over the mountainside.

Congress will probably stay in session until fall. I do not feel that I can leave Lister indefinitely. My plans now are to give up the apartment on July first.

Up to now Congress has done nothing on account of the Court packing plan, and they have a full calendar.

JUNE 1937
2311 CONNECTICUT AVENUE

Thursday morning Dr. Hugo Eckner of Germany, who commands the Graf Zeppelin, appeared before the Military Committee of the House to make a plea for helium. The United States is the only country that produces it. So our country has refused to release it for sale to anyone. Dr. Eckner told Lister, who is the Chairman of the Committee, that unless Germany could obtain helium that they would have to discontinue the transoceanic trips of the Graf Zeppelin and any other lighter-than-air crafts. They only asked for enough helium to inflate these ships on each trip to America, not to exceed three in number. Boake Carter, the news commentator, was there to hear him testify. The Military Committee refused sale of helium to Dr. Eckner.

Lister was very much thrilled over securing the Veterans Hospital for Montgomery. The location in his district caused some unhappiness among a few of his colleagues who wanted it for their districts.

Lister came home the night of July 6, 1937 and announced to me that the Speaker of the House, Will Bankhead, had appointed him as Chairman of the Military Committee, to go to Europe with the Battle Monuments Commission to help dedicate the World War I Monuments which our country had erected in memory of our boys who died in France, Belgium, and England. He was, he said, to sail on Wednesday, July the 14th. That was exactly eight days away. I was flabbergasted! When I had collected my thoughts, I exclaimed, "You need not think you can go without me!"

"Can you make it?" he asked hopefully.

"I will die trying," I said.

I have always been pretty flexible; now I had a real challenge. To begin with there were the two children. They were my first concern. I put in a long distance call to my mother. She readily agreed to keep both children, if I sent the nurse also. Lister called his parents; his mother graciously made the same offer. We decided to send Henrietta to Eufaula with my mother and to let our son remain in Montgomery with Mrs. Hill as our pediatrician would be closer by. The next big hurdle was to get the children to Alabama, close the apartment, pack the children's clothing, get passports and passport pictures, and then there was the small matter of my wardrobe.

The maid and I worked far into the night. We packed the things that were to be stored in Washington until next session, washed windows, waxed floors, packed for the children and then fell into bed.

On Friday we caught the six-thirty train for Alabama. From the station I wired Mr. Al Levy, the owner of a dress shop in Montgomery to send me a selection of dresses to Mrs. Hill's house. The nurse, the two children and I arrived in Montgomery at noon on Saturday. Mama had come over to Montgomery to take Henrietta back home with her to Eufaula. That same day I caught the six-thirty train back to Washington. Mama, Henrietta, and my sister Mary accompanied me to the train to see me off. I had never been separated for any length of time from Henrietta; when the time came to say goodbye she clung to my neck and refused to let go, shrieking. As the train pulled out of the station, I boarded from the back platform. Henrietta broke loose from Mama and started to run after the train. It was the hardest thing I ever did to leave her behind. Someone caught her and held her until the train eased out of sight. It took all the self-control I could muster to keep from leaping off the moving train.

Once I had gone, Henrietta was all right. She spent a very happy summer with my mother. The two of them became great pals. When I returned she had gained ten pounds and was as brown as a berry. I am sure, as she looks back, she is glad that we each had the experiences we did that summer.

Lister and I will stay at the Pennsylvania Hotel in New York both Monday and Tuesday nights. Our ship, the *Manhattan*, sails on Wednesday morning, July 14th, at eleven-thirty. From the cost of my ticket, which was half the price of our cabin, four hundred and fifty dollars, we must have deluxe accommodations. Since Lister is on official business, Uncle Sam pays his fare.

I understand that Ambassador Josephus Daniels (Ambassador to Mexico), who was Secretary of the Navy during the War, and General Benedict Crowell, who was Assistant Secretary of War under Woodrow Wilson, will sail with us.

Our address in Paris will be "American Battle Monuments Commissions, American Government Building, Paris, France." Our hotel there is the St. James and Albany on Rue St. Honoré and Rue de Rivoli. It is best to send mail to the Government Building, as we will be in and out of Paris.

We land at Le Havre, France on July 21st. On July 23rd General Pershing, who is Chairman of the Battle Monuments Commission, will entertain at a reception for our group. I do not know of any other parties as yet.

The first dedication of the World War I Monuments will be held on August first. Our itinerary will include a trip to Brussels and perhaps to Luxembourg. I have long had a desire to see that country.

Mama need never have worried over me being a stranger in a strange land. Lister has two old school mates in Paris. One, Lamar McCann, married a French girl just after the war; the other, Louis Clark of Montgomery, married Ann Covington of Washington. Louis is at present connected with the American Embassy in Paris. When we reach London we expect to see Lister's cousin Dr. Champ Lyons and his wife Naomi, and our old friend Sir St. Clair Thomson.

Wednesday, July 14, 1937
Onboard the *Manhattan*

There is nothing like the excitement of a first voyage on a large ocean liner. I will always remember the gongs ringing, crowds surging, laughter, tears, waving handkerchiefs. Seamen crying, "All ashore that's going ashore!" The steamboat's whistle, the band playing "Sailing, Sailing Over the Bounding Main." The gangplank being raised, stewards wandering about the deck carrying large baskets of flowers and fruit. The Statue of Liberty—a catch in the throat, a tear in the eye—sadness, gladness, but above all, excitement! Then comes a feeling of the majestic grandeur of a ship as it comes alive and begins its prowl proudly into the pathways of the sea.

In spite of all this excitement, there is a tinge of nostalgia as you watch our Lady of Liberty go by. When we were saying farewell to the New York skyline, an elderly gentleman approached us and introduced himself: "I am Josephus Daniels." When we had shaken hands all around, we waved goodbye to the Statue of Liberty. As we did so, Mr. Daniels commented, "The old girl will look mighty good to us when we get back." The three of us chatted for a while before going down to our staterooms. When we arose to depart, Mr. Daniels said, "Mrs. Hill, I understand that you are the ranking lady on board, so you are going to have to look after me; my wife always does, but she couldn't come on this trip."

Mr. Daniels is just as cute as he can be and has a wonderful sense of humor. Everybody on the ship teases him about me. The first night we dressed for dinner he called our stateroom and asked if I was dressed and could he come down to our stateroom. As he entered the door, he said, "Mrs. Hill, I told you that you would have to look after me. Will you please tie my tie? My wife always does." I struggled for a while, then turned him over to Lister.

We have a lovely group of people on board. Traveling with us in our party is Mr. Daniels, General Crowell, Mrs. Baker, Mrs. Boone (Gold Star Mother), John Markey, the Finis Garretts of Tennessee, Dr. Eaton (Congressman of New Jersey), Colonel W.P. Woodside, Vice Chairman of Battle Monuments Commission, Congressman Walter Lambert of North Carolina, Miss Mae Pershing (sister of the General), the Jack Taylors of the American Legion, and Captain Jack Vance—eighteen in all. Also on the ship is Ambassador Hugh Gibson, who is returning to his post as our Ambassador to Belgium. We were glad to renew our acquaintance with Ambassador Gibson as we expect to spend three days in Belgium.

The *Manhattan* is really a beautiful ship. For some reason, I was under the impression that she was old and dilapidated. On the contrary, the *Manhattan* is only three years old, and is a luxury liner. Our stateroom has twin beds, two chests, three closets, and a private bath. There is a swimming pool, a ballroom, and a theatre on the ship.

Our ship lands in La Harve, France, at seven o'clock Wednesday morning, then we go directly to Paris, arriving around noon.

Sunday, July 18, 1937
On Board the *MANHATTAN*

Sailing is such fun! Letters, telegrams, presents, flowers. It was almost like Christmas. Such a comforting feeling to know your friends wish you the best of everything in your adventure.

A number of the members of the Military Committee came up to see us off. They brought me a box with four orchids. Mary sent me a corsage of roses that I wore the first night, saving the orchids for the Captain's dinner on Saturday.

The steward is having a lot of fun with me. He knows that this is my first trip to Europe. When I rang for him to remove the flower boxes and trash, he entered the stateroom, picked up the flower boxes and trash and tossed them out the porthole, saying as he did, "Nobody on the streets at this time of night."

We have a delightful time at our table in the dining room. Ambassador Daniels, Dr. Eaton of New Jersey, Rep. Walter Lambert of North Carolina, the Jack Taylors of the American Legion, and us. The food is excellent. The only trouble is so much to choose from. Jack Taylor starts with "Pâté de Fois Gras and goes through the menu." We have nicknamed him "Pâté." We call Dr. Eaton the "Silver-Maned Stallion," because of his rather shaggy silver hair. The other night when Walter called him that name Dr. Eaton replied, "Oh! Walter, don't call me that, I will begin having nightmares."

After dinner we attend a movie, then dance in the lounge, getting to bed around two o'clock. Every night the clocks are advanced an hour for five consecutive nights which means it is hard to get enough sleep.

One of our party, Col. John Markey of Baltimore, entertained at a cocktail party in his stateroom yesterday before dinner. Being a bit crowded, Mr. Daniels, Mrs. Boone, and I sat on the bed. I kidded Mr. D. by saying, "Mr. Daniels, I bet this is the first time you were ever in bed with three ladies at the same time." Whereupon he roared with laughter.

Mr. Josephus Daniels is one of the most unpretentious men I have ever met. He is very democratic both socially and politically. He is thoroughly loyal to FDR and entirely in sympathy with his program. He loves to tell a good story even at his own expense.

Mr. Daniels told us this story. During the War when he was Secretary of the Navy, he issued General Order No. 99, which dried up the Navy. According to the order, no alcohol was to be allowed on an American ship. At one time an American ship and a British Naval vessel were tied up in the same port. An American officer who was suffering a terrific thirst called on the Admiral of the British Man-of-war. The British Admiral invited the thirsty American to stay for dinner. All during dinner the American officer continued to drink, eating very little. As a consequence, he became very drunk. After dinner, noticing a cellarette in the corner, he asked what it was. The Admiral told him it was where he kept his liquor. The American then noticed an inscription on the cellarette: *God Save the King.* "Why do you have that inscription on here?" the American asked.

"Because," replied the British Admiral, "that reminds the officers of their duty as gentlemen, and to their King."

"That gives me an idea," said the American officer. "When I get back to our ship, I am going to get the biggest hogshead I can find and I am going to write on it, *G.D. Josephus.*" Mr. Daniels is a personal dry.

I overheard someone say that Miss Mae Pershing (the General's sister) was expected to attend the party, so I asked Mr. Garrett to point her out to me when she arrived. "You can't miss her," he said, "she has the same under-slung jaw that the General has." Mr. Garrett was right, Miss Pershing was a massive woman with an under-slung jaw, but very lovely to know.

Wednesday, July 21, 1937
On the Boat Train to Paris

On Tuesday morning at four o'clock we were awakened by boatmen singing "When Irish Eyes are Smiling." I got up and looked out of the porthole and could see a tender approaching the ship from the coast of Ireland to pick up passengers and to bring mail. It was a beautiful sight. Mr. Daniels disembarked for the Emerald Isles and will meet us later in Paris. The same day we arrived at Plymouth, England, at three o'clock in the afternoon, where we put off more passengers and mail. The harbor at Plymouth is a wonderful natural harbor in the shape of a horseshoe.

At six o'clock on Wednesday the steward rapped on our door. "It is time to be up and off," he cried.

Not being dressed, we called, "Who is there?"

"Boots," came the reply.

"Boots?" we asked puzzled. It turned out to be the bootblack whom we had not seen on the entire voyage; nevertheless he was looking for a handout.

Getting off a ship is a pretty expensive business. There is a long line of stewards, stewardesses, etc., etc., all waiting to say goodbye, each with an itching palm.

We did not disembark until nine o'clock. Our passports had to be checked and also our luggage. This was done rather quickly since we were accorded the courtesy of the port.

As I look out of the window from the train, I see the green fields of Normandy, little patches of vegetable gardens which look like a patchwork quilt, every inch of ground under cultivation, rows of tall trees with their lower branches removed (for firewood, I am told), two-wheeled carts, canals and barges, coal and iron factories (Normandy is the industrial section of France). As we approach towns, tall brick houses come into view, every village churches with Norman steeples. Finally, the Cathedral of Rouen looms into view. Here, Joan of Arc was tried and burned at the stake. Now, at last, Paris.

Thursday, July 22, 1937
Paris

· Photographers and reporters and a representative from the Embassy met us on our arrival in Paris. The Military Aide from the Embassy met Lister and me and took charge of our luggage and us. He has placed a car and a chauffeur at our disposal but, knowing Lister, I doubt if he will use it. After being photographed by every photographer in the city we drove to our hotel, the St. James and Albany. The car turned into what appeared to be an alleyway into a courtyard. Our hotel was once a "La Grande Maison." The French are opposed to tearing anything down, so they remodel.

Our hotel room was a distinct shock to me with its red plush carpet, lace curtains, and a huge wardrobe, no closets. Then the bathrooms, for which I am devoutly thankful, are equipped with two washstands, a tin tub, a toilet, and an unmentionable [bidet].

Our bed is brass and has a feather bed on it and a bolster. The sheets, which are very heavy linen, rub off on you. Honestly, they are so stiff I believe they whitewash them.

That afternoon Colonel Waite from the American Embassy came and took us for a drive to give us a view of the city. Paris is the most beautiful city in the world. The French are an artistic nation. Everything is done for beauty's sake. Our hotel faces the Garden of the Tuileries, which, as you may remember, is the Garden of the palace of the French Kings. Now the Louvre. The garden itself is a riot of color. There are more statues in this one garden than in the whole city of Washington. Next, we passed Notre Dame with its apostles being frowned upon by the hideous and grotesque gargoyles, then the Madeline in all of its classical beauty, les Invalides where Napoleon is buried, and the well-known Eiffel Tower. We passed the Exposition then reversed our direction. Men and women sitting out of doors at small tables in front of restaurants. No one in a hurry, there is plenty of time for good living. We drove through the Bois de Boulogne, then back to the Club of the Allies for Tea. The Allies Club was once the residence of the Baron Rothschild; our Army and Navy personnel now use it as a club.

For tea we were served the most wonderful tiny wild strawberries with thick cream and powdered sugar. They were the most delicious strawberries I have ever tasted.

That night we went to bed quite early, too exhausted to go out.

Friday, July 23, 1937

This afternoon we all paid an official call on General Pershing in his private office at the American Embassy. General Pershing, the ex-Commanding General of the A.E.F. has spent most of the past ten years in Paris as the head of the American Battle Monuments Commission.

The General struck me as a bit reserved and dignified. The years have taken their toll, though he still has that wonderful carriage of the soldier.

He furnished his office himself; it is of the Empire period. The walls are blue silk damask with gold stars. His mahogany desk has brass claw feet and the chairs are upholstered in a blue material similar to the wall covering. I suppose that shade of blue is called *French blue*. It is all in very good taste but there are too many stars and too little contrast. I would not have selected it myself.

The General greeted us in a very gracious manner. He is to entertain the men in our party at a stag luncheon on Saturday.

After leaving General Pershing's office, Lister and I went to call on Louis Clark, who was a boyhood playmate of Lister's. Louis is the second Secretary at the Embassy. We talked for a short time then departed for the summer residence of Ambassador Bullitt at Chantilly.

Chantilly is about twenty miles from Paris. The house occupied by our Ambassador is owned by the French Government and is one of the oldest in France. Mr. Bullitt has furnished it beautifully in Louis 15th furniture. I don't think I have ever seen a lovelier garden. It is filled with small picturesque lakes, with beautiful trees and many winding walks. The French are anxious to conserve everything, so Mr. Bullitt had to secure a special permit to fish in the lakes, and a second permit to place a canoe on the lakes for his daughter.

Mr. Bullitt told this tale, which is supposed to be true: buried in the churchyard on the estate is the famous chef of the original owner of the Chateau. The master of the house was to give a dinner one night for some very important people and had promised them a rare treat, "Sole" prepared by his famous chef. The fish was to be brought on donkeys from the seacoast. Hours passed and no fish appeared. When no fish had arrived by the last possible moment in which they could be cooked to perfection, the chef took a butcher knife and plunged it into his heart. As his soul departed, he heard the tinkling of the bells on the donkeys that bore the fish. His body was spirited away while another chef hastily prepared the "Sole."

Thursday night we attended the *Folies Bergére* as the guest of Mr. Daniels. It was one of the strangest experiences we had. Mr. Daniels had asked Capt. Vance to get tickets for himself, for General Crowell, and us for the Opera on Thursday night. Since the Opera season is usually in the wintertime, Capt. Vance was unable to get tickets for it and so substituted tickets to the Follies. I don't believe Mr. Daniels had the least idea where we were going. The opening scene was a mountain brook in which a group of young ladies decided to go swimming, so they took off their clothes and splashed about in the water. The next scene was Josephine Baker with a half costume. I never found out about act three as Mr. D. turned to me in disgust and said, "Let's go."

MONDAY, JULY 26, 1937
PARIS

I spent this morning at the Louvre where I was fortunate enough to hire an English-speaking guide. The French kings used the Louvre for their winter place, and the palace at Versailles in summer. The two things that I liked best in the Louvre were the "Winged Victory" and the "Mona Lisa." The "Winged Victory" has such motion, such strength and power. I was a bit surprised to find the "Mona Lisa" was such a small painting.

This afternoon Lister and I drove out to Fontainebleau, which was the favorite Palace of Napoleon. Architecturally it is very beautiful, though the gardens cannot compare with those at Versailles.

While we were visiting Versailles yesterday the fountains were playing, and that is truly a magnificent sight. We stood on the balcony on which Marie Antoinette watched the angry mob converge upon the Palace and spoke the famous words, "If the people have no bread, why not let them eat cake?"

Sunday morning Louise Taylor and I set out to attend services at the Cathedral of Notre Dame. Unfortunately we had misunderstood the hour of the service and it was almost over before we got there. We then decided to climb the three hundred and seventy-five tiny dark steps up to the tower to make the acquaintance of the gargoyles that grin at you from the eaves. The view from the balcony was magnificent; you could see most of Paris.

THE FRENCH PEOPLE CLOSE their shops at twelve o'clock for the mid-day meal, and keep them closed until two o'clock. They spend this whole time eating. There is no way to hurry the sacred right of eating for a Frenchman. Their service is slow to an American who is used to eating in a hurry. But to a Frenchman, eating is an occasion. Every mid-day meal must include a melon, or a soup, a fish course, meat, vegetables served as a separate course, dessert, then cheese and coffee. It is impossible to get a glass of water. If you are thirsty you drink wine or a bottle of mineral water. I did my best to get a cup of tea, but found it impossible. Dinner is just a repeat of lunch with a few more courses added. It doesn't get dark in Paris, in summer, until nine thirty. We usually dine around eight-thirty. The food is marvelous but too rich for a steady diet. It is no wonder that the French only have coffee and rolls for breakfast; the poor stomach needs a bit of rest. Speaking of coffee, if you can call it such, I drink mine as the French do, with hot milk—that kills some of the chicory taste.

Tomorrow afternoon we are being entertained at a Garden Party given by the President of France.

Next Saturday night we start on our tour of the Battlefields. The first Dedication is to take place on Sunday, August first, at Montfaucon. We return to Paris on Tuesday and will be here until Thursday when we go out again for four days, this time to Brussels.

Tuesday, July 27, 1937
The President's Garden Party

At five o'clock an Embassy car arrived to take Ambassador Daniels and us to the Garden Party which was being given in honor of our group by the President and Madame Blum, at the Palace Elysee.

We had all dressed in our very best attire; the men wore striped pants and cutaways with tall silk beaver hats, while I chose for my costume a short black chiffon over which I wore a white lace jacket. To complete my costume, I wore a large black horsehair garden party hat trimmed in white roses.

Upon our arrival we were announced by a butler and greeted by the President and Madame Blum. Instead of a handshake as we are accustomed to, the ladies all had their hands kissed.

The Blums were very gracious. Mrs. Blum spoke fluent English, but the President not a word. Madame Blum wore a long black dress with a pink organdy bow at the neckline. Around her shoulders hung a black ostrich cape. With greetings over, we were led into the Garden, a very lovely spot, but not as beautiful as our own White House lawn.

Two refreshment tables were placed on the lawn for the guests, with a special table for the President and Madame Blum, General Pershing, Ambassador Daniels, and the rest of us. I sat for a part of the time between General Pershing and the President. On several occasions I had to call on the General to act as interpreter for me. President Blum started the conversation in French with, *"Parlez vous Francais?"* To which I replied in English, with the General to translate. "Your Excellency, I thought I spoke a little French before I came to France, but no one understands even those few words, so I have changed my mind." The President seemed very much amused, as he had recently been in America. We exchanged a few other pleasantries, then a courier arrived with a dispatch and he excused himself for a time, whereupon General Pershing drew a sigh of relief, saying, "That was getting to be a strain on me too."

When the party was over, we wandered back into the Palace through the state dining room. This was a large room filled with Gobelin tapestries hanging from the walls and a dozen pale lavender rock crystal chandeliers, the handsomest I have ever seen.

Wednesday, July 28, 1937
Paris

We have just arrived from a Garden Party that Ambassador Bullitt gave in honor of the American Legion Delegates who have come to France to attend the Dedication Ceremonies and to tour the Battlefields with us. Besides the Legionnaires we have been joined by Senator David Reed of Pennsylvania; Senator Dick Russell of Georgia; Senator and Mrs. Ryan Duffy; Senator Gibson of Vermont; and General John Phillip Hill of Maryland, who is an ex-Congressman.

I wore the same costume as I did yesterday to the Garden Party that the President gave. The women in Paris do not wear pastel clothes in summer, as we do in the South. Mostly, they are poorly dressed and stick to black. Confidentially, I think this is because France is a relatively poor nation, and there are no decent dry cleaning plants. Even the laundry is done by hand, as there are no steam laundries. France is about fifty years behind American in modern conveniences.

Their department stores cannot be compared with ours. The wealthy women have everything custom made and wear the most beautiful clothes in the world.

I am having the most awful time with my high school French. I don't know why Americans don't teach French conversation and let the grammar go. The other day I thought I would have to walk home. I tried three taxi drivers; none them could understand the name of my hotel. Then I got out a piece of paper and wrote *St. James Hotel*. Two of the taxi drivers could not read. These taxi drivers nearly scare you to death they go so fast. I just close my eyes and listen to the *ping-pong, ping-pong* of the horns—and pray.

WEDNESDAY, AUGUST 4, 1937
PARIS

We returned last night from the first group of dedications at Montfaucon, Mont Sec, and Sommes. The dedication of Montfaucon was held Sunday afternoon and was the largest and most important monument to be dedicated. The President of France, Mr. Blum, President Roosevelt, Ambassador Bullitt, General Pershing, and Marshal Petain spoke. Ambassador Bullitt speaks fluent French and has won the hearts of the French people.

It was a very impressive ceremony. President Roosevelt's voice came over the radio from America as clear as if he had been speaking from the platform.

The next afternoon Lister delivered the principal address at Mont Sec. This was the next most important memorial to be dedicated. The setting of the Mont Sec Memorial was far lovelier; it sat right on top of a mountain from which you could view almost a third of France. Lister made a very inspiring speech; in fact he had all the ladies weeping. The men in our party will take turns speaking. Lister's next address will be at the Brookwood Cemetery in England.

I wish the families of the American boys who sleep in these cemeteries could see how beautiful and well kept they are.

General Pershing looked very grand today. He wore his uniform with all of his medals. I couldn't resist asking if he minded my taking his picture. He gave his consent graciously. As I clicked the camera, I remarked, "General, I hope this will be as good looking as you are." He laughed as he said, "Well, they never are."

Our trip to the various battlefields has taken us through much of rural France, which the average tourist seldom sees. We ride a chartered bus most of the time, arising very early and riding until late at night to reach our destination. Most of the battlefields will never again be tillable land; the topsoil has all been destroyed and the people are very bitter over it. Underneath the gaiety of the people is the constant fear of another war.

Each little village we pass through tries to vie with the other in the warmth of their welcome. In many instances, the red carpet is brought out for us to walk upon. They offer us their very best champagne. There are many toasts and speeches, kisses, arms full of roses presented to the ladies, and much good will. Before we depart, we lay a wreath on the monument of their dead heroes.

No matter how small the village in which we dine, the food is always delicious. Captain Vance and Captain Scow (who are in charge of arrangements) ride ahead and prepare the villagers for our coming. They look after our comfort and the little conveniences, which in some cases are negligible.

Mr. Daniels, who is somewhere in his seventies, begins to tire towards evening. He usually sits by me on the bus, for he knows that I will not talk to him when he is tired. I sit and let him nod. These trips are strenuous for all of us.

Our route on this trip took us through Verdun where we spent the night. Next day we visited Belleau Woods and Chateau Thierry. My trip is now a success, as I saw the statue of Jean de La Fontaine, the fabulist, in the square at Chateau Thierry. One of Mama's ancestors, John de La Fontaine, was a French Huguenot who fled to America.

For luncheon yesterday we stopped at Reims. This gave us an opportunity to visit the Cathedral. In front of the Cathedral stands a famous statue of Joan de Arc. It was in this Cathedral that all the French kings were crowned until Napoleon chose the Cathedral of Notre Dame for his coronation.

The Cathedral of Reims is being restored with a grant from the Rockefeller Foundation. The beautiful Rose Window was taken down during the war and buried. It is really magnificent. Many of the other stained glass windows were shattered by German shells.

In the morning we leave for Tours and the Chateau country. I think I will skip the exercises and go sightseeing with several of the ladies. From Tours we take a long jump to Brussels. We return to Paris on the 9th, I think. On the 12th we sail for England where we will be at the Cumberland Hotel in London.

Friday, August 13, 1937
Paris

News has just come of the appointment of Senator Black to the Supreme Court of the United States. We returned to Paris this morning and found three cables stuck under our door. Each said essentially the same thing—*What do you want to do about it?*

Lister paced the floor for a half hour, and then he turned to me and asked, "What about it? What shall I do?"

"It seems to me," I said, "that you have nothing to lose, you won't have to resign your seat in the House, unless you win. You have always wanted to run for the Senate. The longer you wait to announce, the more people will be in the race." And so he sent a cable announcing his candidacy for the Senate.

I am very disappointed that we will have to cut our trip short. We had planned to sail on the 27th, which would have given us ten days in England and Scotland. I hope and pray we will stay in England until the 20th to see a little of that country.

We had a beautiful trip this week through Normandy and Brittany. General Pershing lent his car and chauffeur to Colonel Price to drive to Brest. The Colonel invited us to accompany him on the trip. This was to be the last of the dedications in France. The ride was most enjoyable and was much more comfortable than the bus rides. We spent the first night at Coblentz near Deauville. Colonel Price's wife and children have a house in Deauville for the summer. That evening we dined at a little inn named "William the Conqueror." It was built in the eleventh century and is an old Norman house. The garden was the most beautiful spot I have ever seen. Flowers planted everywhere; it was a riot of color. We went into the kitchen and chose our own lobster. The food was simply superb!

The next day we drove to Bayou to see the famous tapestry made by Matilda, the wife of William the Conqueror in 1056. The tapestry tells the history of the life of William. We found it most interesting. From Bayou we drove to Mont San Michel for luncheon. There was such a crowd of tourists at San Michel that it spoiled the view. We lunched at Madam Poulands, where we enjoyed one of her famous omelets cooked in a copper skillet over hot coals.

Upon our arrival in Brest on Thursday night we changed immediately into evening clothes to attend a banquet given for us by an American who had married a French count, Count de Rodellic du Porgic. The Countess lived in an old Chateau, and was herself eighty-seven. She was all dressed up like a Christmas tree with three strands of pearls, a diamond dog collar, earrings, a diamond tiara, seven bracelets and six rings and an enormous diamond pin. It was a very elegant affair.

My dinner partner that evening was Admiral Darlan, Commandant of the Naval Academy at Brest. I started out talking to the Admiral in English; he nodded and said, "Yes, yes," and I noticed let me do all the talking. I thought by the smiles he gave me that I was certainly making a big hit. The next day at a luncheon at the Naval Academy, I made a dreadful discovery the Admiral had seated me on his right. This time he began the conversation—to my horror, it was entirely in French. In a few moments I recovered my composure and began smiling and nodding, "Oui, oui, oui." It made me think of one of Aesop's fables—the one about the fox and the stork who dined with each other?

We sail for England tomorrow.

OUR TRIP ACROSS THE English Channel was a bit rough, which I was told is not unusual. We arrived in London an hour or so behind schedule, and were taken directly to the American Embassy for a reception, without so much as being allowed to wash our faces. We must have been a pretty dreary looking group of travelers when we shook hands with Ambassador and Mrs. Bingham.

The last of the Dedication Ceremonies of World War I Monuments was held on Sunday afternoon in the Brookwood Cemetery, with Lister making the principal address. I must say he was at his very best and I was indeed proud of him.

Lister and I managed six days in the British Isles before sailing for home on the *Ile de France*. We saw most of the sights in London and spent one day touring the English countryside with Judge and Mrs. Finis Garrett, visiting Windsor Castle, Eaton, and Oxford.

Campaigns & Visitations

The Alabama papers carried a headline: *Lister Hill swims home to start Campaign for the Senate.* Lister spent four weeks in Alabama setting up an organization, then returned to Washington for a short session of Congress. The Alabama Primary was set for January 3, 1938.

JANUARY 10, 1938

I am always hearing Congressmen's and Senator's wives bragging about how they helped elect their husbands to Congress. Lister had been a Member of the House of Representatives for five years before we were married. After his first race for Congress he never had any opposition for his seat in the House. I am afraid I can't take credit for being a help to him in his recent race for the Senate, unless he received a few sympathy votes because of me. On Thanksgiving Day I was admitted to the hospital; after three weeks, I returned home. I had just removed my clothes and crawled into my own bed at home when the maid came running in. "Mrs. Hill, I sure hate to tell you, but the house is on fire." The damage was not too great but the fire put our furnace out of business and the house was icy cold the rest of the day. As a consequence, I caught the flu and did not get up again until Christmas Eve. On my way to the dining room to be with my family, I slipped and broke a finger.

Lister won by a large majority, but it was all due to his own popularity.

We have rented an apartment on Massachusetts Avenue in Washington and will return there soon, in time for Lister to be sworn in as the Junior Senator of Alabama.

APRIL 1938

Henrietta now attends Mrs. Cook's School on Massachusetts Avenue. It is only three blocks from our apartment. Since there are no streets to cross, she walks to school. I chauffeur Lister to the Capitol every day, and then do my marketing on the way home.

Today I am going to the first meeting of a luncheon and sewing club to which I have been elected. It is about the most exclusive organization in the Senate—only eight members. I was very flattered when they invited me to become a member. There has never been anything in the papers about our club. They are all afraid others will get their feelings hurt. Few, if any, of our friends even know of its existence.

My new nurse Nancy is working out very well. She is a good nurse and takes excellent care of the baby and plays with Henrietta in her spare time.

The baby is so active and cute. He can climb out of his bed now. Last night while we were at supper he went into the bathroom and dipped a washrag in the toilet and began scouring the floor. When I came in, he said: "I wash the floor, Mama." He was sopping wet.

Lister goes to Alabama around April 3rd, I think. Wish I could go with him.

SEPTEMBER 1938

POSTSCRIPT TO "MY DAY" ["MY DAY" WAS ELEANOR ROOSEVELT'S DAILY COLUMN IN THE *WASHINGTON POST*]

It was September, and Alabama was in the midst of a drought and a heat wave; no rain had fallen in several weeks. This particular night, there was not a breath of air stirring. You could almost hear the earth sizzling.

As I swung back and forth in the hammock on the porch trying to create a breeze, I heard a familiar "toot, toot," which was Lister's way of warning me that he would be turning into our driveway in a matter of minutes. I was glad to know that he had returned from his trip to North Alabama, but reluctant to leave the hammock.

"How was the trip to Gadsden?" I asked when he entered. "Did you make a good speech? Was the audience responsive?" I need never ask the latter question; I can usually tell by the tone of his voice. Tonight, I was uncertain; he seemed a bit preoccupied. As we sat down to supper in the dining room, he said, "I have a big surprise for you. I will tell you about it after supper." I wasn't too sure it would be a pleasant surprise. He took longer than usual to eat the cold snack I had set before him, and I was dying of curiosity. When the last dish was cleared away, I asked, "What is the surprise?"

Lister cleared his throat, then proceeded cautiously. "As I was checking out of the hotel in Gadsden, I ran into Mrs. Roosevelt, who was just arriving. She is scheduled to speak tonight to the same audience I addressed this afternoon. We chatted and I told her I regretted not being able to hear her speak, but that we were looking forward to hearing her tomorrow night here in Montgomery, when she speaks at the City Auditorium. Then she told me she was due to arrive in Montgomery on the afternoon train, but if possible she would prefer to arrive on the ten o'clock in the morning and drive over to see Tuskegee Institute. Did I think it could be arranged?" There was a pause, and then came the bolt from the blue. "I have invited her to be our house guest and to have luncheon with us tomorrow."

I was stunned! For a few seconds I could not speak. Finally I said, "Lister, you are joking. You couldn't have. Have you taken a look at this house? The painters just left this afternoon and the place is a mess. All the curtains are down, pictures packed away, and stacks of books are all over the floor. Not to mention that we have no cook."

"I am sorry," he said apologetically, "there is no way out. Spend whatever you have to and I will pay for it."

That made it sound simple enough, only where do you find a cook at eight o'clock at night? How do you prepare for a visit from the First Lady with your house in this condition? While I was pondering these problems, Lister put in a long distance call for Mrs. R., then handed me the receiver, saying, "You should confirm my invitation."

Mrs. R. was most gracious, insisting that I go to no trouble, but requesting an early luncheon since she was extremely anxious to make the tour to Tuskegee.

As soon as I had hung up the receiver, I grabbed the car keys and dashed out of the house. "Where are you going?" called Lister.

"To find a cook!" I replied.

The one person I knew who could really do the job properly was a woman named Mattie, who had once worked for my sister-in-law Amalie Hill Laslie (Lister's twin sister). I sallied forth into the night in the direction of the Negro district, without the faintest idea where Mattie lived. I had heard she had recently moved, perhaps within the same neighborhood. In those days, an address would have been of little help anyway. The colored population were said to choose any number that suited them, and if they moved they took their number with them. It made no difference if several persons had the same numerals tacked on their door, on the same street.

I turned onto the street where Mattie had last lived, hoping perhaps one of her neighbors could furnish me some information as to her whereabouts. I stopped the car, blew the horn, and shouted "Mattie!" Two figures in different houses across the street answered "Mam." One was a tall mulatto woman dressed in a flowered kimono, the other a dark, stout woman. The mulatto went back into the house, apparently annoyed at being disturbed; the dark, fat woman replied to my inquiry: "No'me, I don't believe I knows her."

I tried the next block, honking the horn and shrieking "Mattie!" Finally, I came across a teen-aged girl who asked, "Do you mean Mrs. Laslie's Mattie? Yessum, she moved last summer, just around the corner. I think she lives next door to Belle the Milker." At last I located the right Mattie, the woman I hoped would cook Mrs. R. the best dinner she had ever eaten. Mattie was delighted at the prospect to demonstrate her talents, and promised to be at my house next morning at six o'clock.

The rest of the night, Willie May (our baby's nurse) and I spent trying to bring some sort of order out of all that chaos. We washed windows, hung curtains and pictures, and rearranged the books on the shelves. At three o'clock I fell into bed too exhausted and too excited to sleep. With the first crack of dawn there was a faint tapping at the kitchen door and I drew a sigh of relief that Mattie had not let me down.

While Mattie set the table, I went to the farmer's market for vegetables and chickens. An hour later, I was back, loaded down with paper sacks and arms full of flowers. At nine, Lister drove down to the station to meet Mrs. R. while we completed the household chores. By the time our distinguished guest arrived, everything was in perfect order—a feat of which I have always been exceedingly proud.

Mrs. Roosevelt was accompanied on her travels by her secretary, Miss Malvina Thompson, whom she called "Tommie." It was to Tommie she dictated her column, "My Day," though I wondered afterwards when the dictation took place.

We sat down to luncheon almost immediately. Dining with us that day were Lister's mother Mrs. L.L. Hill, his sister Amalie Laslie, and our eight-year-old daughter Henrietta. Although we had cautioned Henrietta not to tell her friends of Mrs. R.'s presence in the neighborhood, I am afraid she could not resist the temptation since there was a continuous series of children's heads bobbing up and down at the windows.

Mattie had every reason to be proud of the luncheon she served us, but I doubt if Mrs. R. had the vaguest idea what was set before her, so intent was she in ferreting out information to take back to the President. The conversation centered principally on the problems of the day, and particularly in Alabama. The First Lady seemed far more interested in causes than in personalities.

We had barely risen from the table when Mrs. Frank Dixon, our Governor's wife, arrived in the state limousine to take us on a tour of central Alabama. From the minute we were seated in the limousine, the events of the day will always remain a bit of a jumble to me. This was my first experience driving at ninety miles an hour accompanied by a police escort with sirens going full blast.

Our group arrived at our first stop, Tuskegee, in a big cloud of dust. After we had viewed the campus of the Institute we were escorted into the auditorium to hear the famous choir of Tuskegee Institute sing spirituals. Then the music from their melodious voices drifted away and we were back on the highway headed for Auburn University, ten miles away. Here, Mrs. R. was greeted by five thousand cheering students. The thunderous voices ceased when it became apparent that the First Lady would speak. "I am particularly glad to see what the Federal Government had to do with the progress of this institution." Then the cheers rose again, for the students knew that she referred to the million and a half dollars expended by the Government through WPA building programs. The students were there to express their appreciation in no uncertain terms. The President of the Student Council then presented Mrs. R. with a bunch of American Beauty roses. As the limousine drove away Mrs. R. called, "Thank you for a grand welcome."

So rapidly were we whisked about the state, I began to feel that we were riding on a magic carpet. Three o'clock found us back at home with just enough time allotted to change into an afternoon dress, to attend a reception at the Governor's Mansion. Here we shook hands with the state legislators and their wives. Before anyone could offer us refreshments, we were bidding goodbye to the Governor and his lovely wife. Dinner awaited us twenty miles away, in Autauga County, at the plantation home of Col. Hobson Owen Murphy—a delightful, cultured gentleman of the old South. Colonel Murphy had been a regular correspondent of Mrs. R. for a number of years; his charming letters had enticed her to accept his hospitality should she ever visit Alabama.

We were quickly introduced to the guests, and just as quickly seated at the table of the spacious dining room, where an elaborate meal awaited us. Halfway through the main course I glanced up in time to see Mrs. Roosevelt arise and bid our host goodnight. The amazed servants rushed to the kitchen to bring in the "piece de resistance," the dessert—but we could linger no longer.

Back in Montgomery again, we made a quick change into formal attire for the evening lecture. When Mrs. R. walked out onto the stage she looked as fresh as if she had been lying in my hammock all day. Her evening dress was most becoming, fashioned of black velvet and cut fairly low in the neckline to display her lovely white shoulders. I was deeply impressed by her poise and dignity, though I confess that I was so tired that I shall never know what she said, other than that it had something to do with the problems of youth. The lecture concluded, we accompanied Mrs. R. and Miss Thompson to a reception given in her honor at the home of Mrs. Roland Nachman, the then-president of the PTA. Around twelve o'clock we bid farewell to the indefatigable Mrs. R. at the railway station and turned wearily homeward. Utterly exhausted, we fell into bed.

I suppose I might have slept around the clock the next day had not Willie May brought me a cup of coffee with the morning *Advertiser*. On the front page appeared an article entitled "Call at Montgomery Gives Mrs. Roosevelt a Full Day." I turned over and might have gone back to sleep when Henrietta came into my room and handed me a clipping. "Daddy said to give you this." The article was written by our guest of the day before, under the byline "My Day." Underscored in red ink were these lines, "Yesterday was one of the most strenuous days of my life." I picked up a pencil and wrote *P.S.* at the bottom of the clipping, then the words "Amen! . . . What a day!"

APRIL 19, 1939

My cold is about gone and I am feeling fine again. The Seventy-Fifth Club (a congressional organization whose name comes from the session number of the Congress to which a person is elected) gave a luncheon for Mrs. Roosevelt. The Club President, Mrs. William T. Byrne, sat on Mrs. Roosevelt's left. As I am the vice president I sat on Mrs. Roosevelt's right. She is really quite a person. After the luncheon, Mrs. Jon Murdock, a former President, introduced Mrs. Roosevelt, who gave an informal talk on her trip to the west and the Fair in San Francisco. The money we took in from the luncheon was given to one of Mrs. Roosevelt's favorite charities, Francis Lansdale, a student at Langdon School for crippled children. Nearly two hundred members and guests attended.

The Seventy-Fifth Club's interest in Francis Lansdale began three years ago when it became known his wheelchair had been stolen. We purchased a chair and presented it to him in the name of Mrs. Roosevelt. Since then the Club has continued its aid to the boy and yesterday made a gift towards his education in honor of the First Lady. Mrs. Jerry Vories announced this.

It is doubtful that the King and Queen of England will visit this country on account of conditions in Europe, but as yet their trip has not been cancelled. The people who are invited to meet the King and Queen will be invited because of position only. I think I have been here long enough to be invited at least to a reception, if not to a dinner.

MAY 1939
2540 MASSACHUSETTS AVENUE, N.W.

Every Thursday I try to stay home and serve tea to anyone who calls. Last Thursday I had twelve callers and served them nut bread sandwiches, which they seemed to enjoy.

Little Lister fell out of his bed last Sunday night and broke his collarbone, but we did not discover he had a fracture until yesterday. The first doctor who saw him said he was just bruised. The child kept suffering so much that I took him to a bone specialist for x-rays. He will have to wear an uncomfortable brace for three weeks, but his pain has ceased. Today he is quite cheerful. He can go out in the car and can play. We do have to watch him carefully. He was as good as gold when I took him to the hospital, never cried a minute, just stood up like a little man and let the doctor fix him.

Lister is out at a stag dinner tonight for Justice Frankfurter, the last appointee on the Court. It looks as if Bill Douglas or Senator Schwellenbach will be appointed to the latest vacancy. At any rate it will be a westerner.

I went to luncheon for a very charming Belgium prince, who was a relative of the King's, named Prince De Linge. He is coming to lunch with Lister and me at the Capitol on Tuesday.

MAY 1939

I bought a new hat today. It is white and is covered all over with white flowers, with a veil which twines around the neck like a scarf. It is really adorable. It will be my best hat all summer.

Thursday, I am hostess for the Senate Ladies Luncheon Club. It is an organization formed of wives of the members of the Senate. They meet each Tuesday to do Red Cross work and have a luncheon afterwards. This organization was formed on April 18, 1917, during World War I, at the Willard Hotel, and has continued in existence ever since. Mrs. Key Pittman of Nevada was chosen first President.

Each member of the Club has to serve as a hostess twice a year. There are seven other ladies on the committee with me. I am donating a Virginia ham, and certainly do hate to part with it. It was cooked yesterday and smells so good. Mrs. Jack Garner, our Vice President's wife, is President of the Senate Ladies. Mrs. Garner introduced me to Mrs. W.H. Smathers of New Jersey. "You are the only two young things I know," she said.

We are going out tomorrow night for a dinner for Felix Frankfurter, the newest member of the Supreme Court.

The King and Queen of England are actually on their way to America. I suppose I will have a chance to see them some place while they are in Washington.

I HAVE NEVER KNOWN anything like the excitement over the coming visit of King George and Queen Elizabeth of England. For weeks before their arrival there were speculations as to who would be invited to the Garden Party given by the British Ambassador and Lady Lindsey, and who would not.

I don't think it ever occurred to the wives of the Members of the Senate that they would not all be included in the guest list. Three or four weeks before the event, I was at a luncheon where a number of Senate wives were present. Invitations had just been received in the morning's mail. The majority of the ladies had not received invitations; the lucky few were jubilant over their prizes and spent the luncheon hour discussing whether they should wear a long or a short dress, and whether it was proper for Americans to curtsey or shake hands with Royalty. The uninvited sat—unhappily—and listened.

I don't know why Americans get so excited over Royalty, unless it is a hangover from the fairy tales we hear as children.

The uninvited press was likewise in an uproar, for they knew that their reading public would want every last little detail of the Royal visit. Eventually Ambassador Lindsey capitulated, rumor says, because of a directive from the Prime Minister of England, to "invite all members of Congress and the press, regardless of space."

Our invitation came on the second go round. Only Chairmen of Committees had been included in the beginning. The invitation reads thus:

The British Ambassador
Has received Their Britannic Majesties Commands
to invite, Senator Lister Hill
and Mrs. Hill
to a Garden Party at the Embassy
on Thursday, the 8th of June 1939

Here is my reply:

Mrs. and Mrs. Lister Hill have the honor
to accept the invitation extended by
The British Ambassador at their
Britannic Majesties Commands to a Garden Party
at the Embassy on Thursday
the 8th of June 1939

I wore a long dress and a large garden party hat with pink roses on it. About half of the ladies came in long dresses; the others wore short dresses. Three-fourths of the men appeared in striped trousers and cutaway coats. A few sensible ones wore white suits.

June 8th turned out to be one of those humid insufferable days in which you can scarcely breathe. The poor men in cutaways nearly died of the heat; their collars were all wilted. The garden at the Embassy, which is a rather large one, was so packed with people you could scarcely move. The King and Queen wandered about the garden shaking hands with some person now and then, but mainly the Royal Couple paraded about for all to catch a glimpse of them.

About forty minutes after the affair started, it began to sprinkle and their majesties retired, and most of the guests departed. With few exceptions the guests went home thoroughly content, for now they could explain to their constituents that they had seen the King and Queen of England; they were important enough to have been included in the party—and thus, everybody was made happy.

On the night before the Garden Party, the King and Queen were entertained at a dinner at the British Embassy. Our apartment on Massachusetts Avenue is only three blocks from the Embassy. Just before time for the King and Queen to pass our apartment on their way to dinner, the streets were lined with policemen who cleared all traffic. When the King and Queen rode by, Her Majesty looked every bit the storybook queen. She wore a pale pink tulle evening gown sprinkled with brilliants. On her head she wore a diamond tiara. There was so much warmth in her greeting, her smile and dainty little wave of her hand, that she quite captivated all who saw her. Seeing her gave our children a thrill.

The visit of their majesties to the U.S. proved that the British Commonwealth accepts the U.S. as a world power.

JANUARY 1940
WARDMAN PARK HOTEL

It is warmer now and the snow has begun to melt. I hope we won't have any more really deep snows.

I am so glad Lister and I saw *Gone With the Wind*. It is a wonderful production. We enjoyed it immensely.

Lister did not feel like going to the White House reception on Thursday night, so I went with Senator and Mrs. Morris Sheppard of Texas. This reception was for the military and is considered one of the most colorful of all the receptions. There are several others, the Naval, Diplomatic, Congressional, and Judicial.

The most interesting person I met at the reception that night was Eve Curie, the daughter of Madam Curie who discovered radium. I had recently read *Madam Curie* and had enjoyed it so much. Mlle. Curie was stunning looking with her coal black hair and blue eyes. She wore a deep blue dress with several tiers of bustles down the back.

Henrietta starts to school Monday. I hope it will not be too difficult for her. Taking her in and out of schools each year is hard on the child. Last year she complained that she had studied Africa in her geography course three times, but had never studied Europe. It is frightfully expensive sending her to private schools but it is the only way she can pretend to keep up with moving so often.

FEBRUARY 15, 1940
WARDMAN PARK HOTEL

We are moving in a few days to another apartment at 2540 Mass. Avenue. It is the same building we have lived in before, only this time we have a larger and nicer apartment. It is a lot of trouble to have to move but we do not like having the children in a hotel apartment.

Our new apartment has three bedrooms and two baths. We have been so cramped in a two-bedroom apartment with one bath. The living room is quite large, and has a real fireplace, which we will enjoy.

Henrietta is crazy about her new school. I can't tell you what a relief it is to have someone amuse her all afternoon; she was miserable with no children to play with. It is harder on the children of Congressional families than on anyone else. Henrietta always weeps for at least a half hour every time we leave Montgomery. She hates to give up her little friends. Then there is the adjustment in changing schools in mid-term each year.

I had the hardest time explaining to Henrietta and Lister Junior why I could not bring the dollhouse and the fire truck to Washington with us. These were their favorite Christmas toys.

Lucy George says her son Marcus was always miserable in Washington, because there was no place for him to play baseball.

Washington has many advantages, but try and explain that to a child.

EASTER 1940

We had a terribly cold day for Easter Sunday. All of those who bought new Easter outfits were out of luck and could not wear them. Lister and Henrietta went to Alabama for a week's visit. I have Lister Junior and Willie Mae here to keep me from getting lonely.

I am working on a tea for the Alabama DARs for this spring. The entire Alabama delegation is going to give it jointly. It will be quite a large affair at the Democratic Club.

The Joe Lyons family (Lister's maternal uncle) has been in town for a few days. They have always been so nice to us; it is a pleasure to have them here.

I am taking Lister Junior to the Children's Service this afternoon at St. Johns Church. After that I am going with Helen Newton to a tea at Bolling Field. The hostess is from Montgomery and married into the Air Corps.

We have an engagement for dinner with the Bankheads next week; it is in honor of Uncle Joe and Aunt Olive. Uncle Joe and John Bankhead are great friends.

Last Sunday night, Lister and I entertained the Alben Barclays of Kentucky (Leader of the Senate), Senator and Mrs. Claude Pepper of Florida (both born in Alabama), Mrs. Gilbert Hitchcock (widow of Senator Gilbert Hitchcock), and the French Ambassador, Count San Quentin.

I let little Henrietta dress up in her long party dress and come in and speak to the guests. She had a grand time talking to the French Ambassador in French. I couldn't help envying her ability to make herself understood in a foreign language.

I went to another lovely party this week which Mrs. Henry Wallace (wife of Secretary of Agriculture) gave. Wallace is running as hard as he can for the Presidential nomination. Mrs. Wallace had the Swiss Minister's wife, Mary Bruggman (her sister-in-law), the Chilian Minister's wife and the Norwegian Ambassador's wife, Madam Morgansteirne (a lovely person), also Mrs. W.O. Douglas (wife of Supreme Court Justice Douglas) and a number of the press.

Everybody here talks of nothing but war, Finnish relief, the French homeless and Presidential candidates.

June 25, 1940

The children and I are off this morning to Atlantic City, and we will be gone until Sunday. Lister had to go to Mississippi to Pat Harrison's funeral and will come back by way of Alabama. When Mary Jim Smathers, wife of Senator William Smathers of N.J., called and invited us over to Margate, N.J., we were all delighted. Both children are terribly excited over going to the beach.

On Tuesday Henrietta leaves for Rock Brook Camp, at Brevard, N.C. Lister Junior and I will leave the next day for Alabama. We sent our dog Champ by express to Mr. Watts Kennels, where we bought him. He will board there until we are home again. He is a sweet, affectionate cocker. Champ is like a member of the family; he sleeps at the foot of our son's bed, which is a grand protection for him.

Calling the Roll

About a week before Lister left for Chicago and the Democratic Convention, Harry Hopkins telephoned and invited him to come down to the White House to talk about the Convention. Alabama being the first on the roll call occupies a strategic position.

Lister was ushered into the Emancipation Room, the room in which Lincoln signed the Emancipation Proclamation. "How would you like to nominate FDR for the presidency for a third term?" Harry asked Lister.

Lister was sworn to secrecy—in fact, he never told me that tale until twenty-five years later. He was thrilled over being chosen to nominate the first President for a third term in the history of our country. Lister went to Chicago several days before the Convention started. I followed, arriving the first day of the Convention.

July 14, 1940
Enroute to Democratic Convention in Chicago
Dear Mama,

I started out to the platform of the train to tell you there were five people I knew in my car, when the train pulled out. The Ed Leigh Mc-Millians from Brewton, (they are close friends of Lister's), the Maynors, and Pitt Tyson Maynor, all of Montgomery.

I am enclosing a clipping from tonight's *Alabama Journal*, which I bought in the station. It is under Drew Pearson's column, "Washington Merry-Go-Round." Since Alabama is first on the roll call, Lister will be the first person to answer his name. Don't be surprised if he makes a speech.

Incidentally, there is a good-looking young man across the aisle from me. Being a well brought up young lady, I remember you said, "Don't ever talk to strangers." However, he is doing his best to get acquainted.

I found an amethyst ring in the ladies room a while ago. It later turned out to belong to Mrs. McMillian.

This will be my first political convention. It ought to be a lot of fun.

Love, H.

MORRISON HOTEL
CHICAGO

For the first three days and nights, neither Lister nor I was able to sleep very much, in spite of the fact that we had comfortable quarters. The telephone rang day and night. There was an air of excitement so thick, so tense in Chicago that hot summer week of the 1940 Democratic Convention that we found it extremely difficult to relax at all. At four o'clock the morning of the day before FDR was to be nominated, the telephone rang. Harry Hopkins requested Lister to come to his hotel suite at the Stevens Hotel. I did not see Lister again until late morning; he looked ghastly.

WHEN THE CONVENTION HAD been called to order and all necessary business dispensed with, the Chairman, Senator Barkley, announced, "The Clerk will now call the roll. Alabama."

[The following is an extract from pages 166-167 of the *Official Proceedings of the Democratic National Convention*.]

THE READING CLERK (Mr. Emory Frazier, Kentucky): Alabama.

THE HONORABLE LISTER HILL (Alabama): Alabama desires to make a nomination.

THE PERMANENT CHAIRMAN: The Chair is advised that the State of Alabama desires to submit a nomination, and the spokesman for Alabama will please come to the rostrum.

The Chair takes pleasure in recognizing the brilliant young junior Senator from the State of Alabama, the Honorable Lister Hill. (Applause.)

[FRANKLIN D. ROOSEVELT PLACED IN NOMINATION BY SENATOR LISTER HILL, OF ALABAMA]

THE HONORABLE LISTER HILL (Alabama): Mr. Chairman, Fellow Democrats: We meet not merely to answer our party's call but to answer the call of America in the hour of her need.

The Alabama delegation places its duty to our country above and beyond all selfish aims. Our delegation at first desired to place in nomination that illustrious son of Alabama, the Temporary Chairman of this convention, the Speaker of the House of Representatives, who has been the strong right arm in the House of Representatives of the present Democratic Administration. But that desire is overwhelmed by the desire shared by the Speaker himself to put service to our country first. (Applause and cheers.)

America needs loyal hearts today more than she has ever needed them in all her history.

This is no time for untried hands to pilot the Ship of State. (Applause and cheers.)

This convention must name a leader whose record of achievements will inspire our nation with supreme confidence.

Fortunately for us and for our country, we have in our party a man with courage beyond all question, who came back from a living death to serve his country (applause) and with a proven will to live and to achieve. The greatness of his vision is demonstrated by the roll of his achievements.

When the great banks and bankers of America were falling before a force beyond all their power and beyond all their efforts to withstand, this man saved them.

When millions of Americans, faint with hunger, cried out in their anguish, he gave them food. When strong hearts grew faint, he gave them courage.

Under his leadership a nation living in gloom became a resolute people marching towards the light of a better day and of a better world.

His heart made him the friend of the lowly. His deeds show him to be the friend of all, both great and small. With such a man in our party there is no choice left to us. He alone is strong enough to match the strength of America against the avalanche of fate. If peace is possible, and I pray Almighty God that it is, he can preserve it for us, and he will. (Applause and cheers.) If war is inevitable, he can win it for us and he will.

If America is to survive, we must all give the best that there is in us and must demand the best of every American. We must be valiant and we must demand valor.

The man whose name I am proud to offer saw the approach of the whirlwind of disaster while it was yet far off. He has labored to make us strong, to keep us at peace and to keep us free. He stands forth the symbol of the hopes of all the stricken and suffering peoples upon this earth.

In the name of the people of the State of Alabama, in the name of the people of the whole United States and in furtherance of the cause of freedom and law and justice, in a world that is gripped with chaos, I place in nomination [that] valiant American, Franklin Delano Roosevelt. (Applause and cheers.)

. . . There was a demonstration which began at 9.55 o'clock and continued to 10.17 . . .

THE NEXT DAY, FLORENCE Bankhead, wife of the Speaker of the House of Representatives, Matilee Grant and I attended a luncheon at Mrs. Edward O'Neal's. On our way back to the hotel, Florence invited us to stop by her room. Minutes before, Franklin Roosevelt had called the Speaker of the House, Will Bankhead, in his suite in Chicago. Before the Speaker could cool off, we walked into his room. Bankhead was still furious. I shall never forget the scene when he related to his wife the conversation with FDR. The exact words I have forgotten but they were to this effect: "Well, Florence, the President just called and asked me to come down and not to make the race for the Vice Presidency. After promising me he would stay out of the race for VP he has chosen Wallace as his running mate. I told him that I was staying in."

The other candidates all came down with the exception of Bankhead, who stayed in the race to the finish. The nomination for the VP was no more of a farce than at any other Convention for the vice presidency. The President always named his own running mate. Any candidate who has strength enough to be nominated president, likewise, can muster that same strength for any designated running mate.

Being on the inside of many of the conferences, I can truthfully say that Bankhead lucked out of a bad situation. The poll on the eve of the nomination for Vice President showed Bankhead to have only fifty votes—he had run in an open field against McNutt, Jimmie Byrnes, Sam Rayburn, Henry Wallace, Jim Farley, and a score of lesser contenders. Every state had a favorite son: Claude Pepper of Florida, Jessie Jones of Texas, Clyde Herring of Iowa, Leon Henderson, Jack Garner, all hoped for the lightning to strike them. Some of these candidates came down ungraciously. Unforgivingly, they threw their strength to Bankhead. For a split second it looked like a tie.

JULY 15, 1940
MORRISON HOTEL, CHICAGO

I am sitting on my bed in the hotel room, too exhausted from excitement to sit at the desk, yet too wide awake to go to sleep. I have just witnessed a most remarkable and historic scene—a wild, uncontrolled demonstration for President Roosevelt's nomination for a third term to the highest office in the land!

It was Lister who had the privilege of breaking the age-old precedent of two terms for a president by nominating Franklin Roosevelt for a third term.

The scene keeps passing before me, indelibly impressed upon me for all times—I see crowds of cheering throngs milling around, people from each state in the Union carrying banners. There goes North Carolina with a banner: "26 votes for Roosevelt." A Texas hat poised on a stick in absence of a banner. The state flag of Pennsylvania. A Panama hat on top of the Canal Zone banner. Waving corn from the state of Iowa. Noise, whistles, an organ playing in the background, bedlam—the complete abandon of a frenzied crowd!

As I look back on this Convention, my first, I can never forget the drama which was played before my eyes—Paul McNutt three times trying to tell the crowd that he renounced the crown. The deafening uproar, which arose in a vocal *No, No, No.* Iola Wallace's tears when Henry was booed. The disappointment of Will Bankhead when he learned that he had been passed over as a Vice Presidential nominee.

A convention is like a three-ring circus.

Men stay up all night and swap and trade candidates. A convention is one of the great dramas of America. No matter whether you approve of their selections or not, you still have a chance next time to make a change in this Democratic process. Vive la Conventions!

One of the most dramatic moments of the Convention came on the fourth night, when the vice president was to be nominated.

The Vice Presidential nominee we all knew would be chosen by FDR and the procedure would be short and to the point. Against everybody's advice, Harry Hopkins was determined to have it over with on the first ballot.

The vice presidential candidate had always been picked by the presidential nominee, and is usually a cut and dried affair, after being decided by trading at the local convention headquarters. Henry Wallace's selection was no more of a farce than the Vice President of a dozen other Conventions—only the technique was poorly manipulated.

Each candidate or favorite son is usually allowed to run a ballot or two to save his face and to give a legitimate air to the convention. On this occasion, realizing the jig was up, they began to gracefully retire from the field. The most dramatic moment came with Paul McNutt (a former National Commander of the American Legion and the ex-Governor of the Philippines) rose to withdraw his name. If ever a man looked beautiful, he did. The tall, iron gray haired man was truly magnificent to behold when he arose to push the crown from him. There were shouts of "No! No! No!" so deafening that the Speaker could not be heard. The words, which he had resigned himself to say, were lost in the tumult. In vain he pleaded; the shouts grew louder: "No, No." The noise arose higher and higher and continued for twenty minutes. A bitter cup for McNutt to take—but no one can be nominated by the shouts from the galleries. There were times when McNutt looked desperate when he shouted, "Please." He seemed to wish it over and done with.

Now came the roll call of the states—Alabama, and then down the list. The race, which no one expected, began. Enough of the favorite sons and disappointed candidates threw their votes to Will Bankhead as a protest, nearly upsetting the apple cart.

I can still hear the boos. The same voices that had shouted "No" to Paul McNutt a few moments prior now joined in booing Wallace every time his name was mentioned. Mrs. Wallace dissolved in tears and sat frozen upon the speakers' platform.

Tall green corn flown in from Iowa began waving about on the Convention floor. The Alabama delegation could be seen wandering the aisles, looking for strength for Bankhead. Then the roll call continued; it began to look as if the anti-Roosevelt/pro-Bankhead followers could throw a bomb into the well-laid plans to nominate Wallace as running mate of FDR.

There is something that gets into your blood at a convention. I never dreamed that I would get out and march when the Alabama delegation began to demonstrate for Bankhead. Someone stuck a banner in my hand and off I went. I knew then that it was a losing fight but I was proud of our candidate and of Alabama. So march I did for the glory of Alabama.

I asked one lady next to me why she booed Henry Wallace—did she know him? "No," she answered, but the rest of the crowd was doing it and she thought it looked like fun. Mass psychology in a huge gathering is contagious. I even booed somebody myself before the evening was over. Booing is like the seventh inning in a baseball game: the seats get hard late at night, and I discovered it was a wonderful outlet for an emotional turmoil. Thank God we have Conventions—as clumsy as they are, they still work.

Lister, Henry Steagall, and I shared a taxi back to the Morrison Hotel after the adjournment for the night. "Bankhead will never know how lucky he was," said Steagall. "I polled delegates this morning and found that we only had fifty votes pledged to him. This way Alabama was duly honored and Bankhead came out of the Convention a far bigger man than he was before."

PART TWO

1941–1943

Days of Infamy

I n the valley of the Tennessee River on the Alabama side is a town
known as Listerhill, Alabama. I saw it when it was just an excavation.
The name was chosen as a gesture and a thank you from Richard S.
Reynolds, Sr., the CEO of Reynolds Metals.

One day in 1940, Reynolds walked into Lister's office. "Senator, what
can I do to help my country? The war clouds are gathering and I would
like to do whatever I can to help."

Lister thought for a moment. "Mr. Reynolds, are you prepared to go
into the aluminum business? The greatest need, in my mind, is aluminum
for building airplanes. We need air power desperately."

Mr. Reynolds was so inspired that he went home to take stock of all
his holdings, to figure a way to raise the money to go into the aluminum
business. He ended by mortgaging all his property, running a risk that
few people are willing to take.

How right Lister and Mr. Reynolds had been. The Reynolds Metals
Company contributed tremendously to the winning of World War II.

Whenever I now wrap Christmas gifts with the charming peacetime
production of the Reynolds Metals Company, I am grateful that we
have peace.

MEMORIAL EXERCISES, 1941

Mrs. Will Bankhead, the widow of the former Speaker of the House
of Representatives, was in town to attend the Memorial Exercises for
her late husband. Will Bankhead was beloved by everyone and was
considered the fairest and most just Speaker the House has had in many
generations.

The Memorial Exercises are held once a year at the Capitol by the

Joint Houses of Congress, for the deceased members of the House and Senate who have died during the past year. On this occasion there were nine Representatives and four Senators mourned. The Senators were: Key Pittman of Nevada (the Chairman of the Foreign Affairs Committee and President Pro Tempore of the Senate); Morris Sheppard of Texas (author of the Prohibition Act); Ernest Lundeen (killed in a plane crash); and Senator Gibson of Vermont (who died of old age, a rarity in Congress).

Attending the exercises with Mrs. Bankhead were the Speaker's daughter Eugenia and her husband William Sprouce, and Mr. and Mrs. Tom Owens (Mr. Owens was a nephew of the deceased). The Speaker's other daughter, Tallulah, was unable to be present.

I had a short talk with Mrs. Bankhead before she left town. She is trying very hard to adjust to her life.

(A year later, I saw her in the lobby of the Mayflower Hotel—by then a broken soul, lost and bewildered. We sat for an hour and I listened to the sad lament of a woman who by nature is a clinging vine. Left alone with no one to cling to, she had to learn to write a check, and was attempting to run a farm and to raise cattle and specimen tomatoes. On the side, she sculpts. The sum total of her life is misery; she told me that the last two years before Billy died, she was afraid to let him out of her sight. He had an enlarged aorta and it was her constant fear something would punch him in the stomach. He was totally unaware that his condition was that serious. I jotted this down while it was still fresh in my mind, for there had been much discussion over the apparent double cross of Will Bankhead at the Chicago Convention. This re-evaluation, however, bears out my former suspicion that Will Bankhead was not physically fit to serve as Vice President. Of this, I am convinced, FDR was fully aware—and Will Bankhead died just two months after the Democratic Convention.)

Her daughter Eugenia Bankhead's husband is in the Marines, and is detailed to the White House. They are newlyweds and are honeymooning in a trailer. That is one way to beat the housing shortage.

Since the Memorial Exercises three days ago, two other Senators have died: Pat Harrison of Mississippi, and Sam Houston of Texas (son of the famous Texan). It is surprising that the percentage of deaths in Congress isn't higher. These men live under constant pressure and tension. The past session of Congress was the longest in history. This coming session will no doubt be just as long, and will probably merge into the next one.

Unless I miss my guess, Kenneth McKeller of Tennessee, a native born Alabamian, will be elected to fill Pat Harrison's place as President Pro Tempore of the Senate. Lister, who has been presiding over the Senate all during Pat's long illness, is already the Democratic Whip. Altogether there are five native born Alabamians in the Senate. Besides Lister and McKeller, there are Claude Pepper of Florida, John Bankhead, and Josh Lee of Oklahoma. (Alabama is well represented in the upper chamber.)

Senator Alben Barkley, the Majority Leader of the Senate, has been ill and has been recuperating at Atlantic City, N.J., as the guest of Senator and Mrs. W. H. Smathers. The Smathers report that the Senator is doing fine. The other day he went in the ocean twice, then finished off by doing a sprint down the beach—just to prove that he could.

JUNE 1941

Dearest Mama,

I have been sick with the flu but have now recovered and am out again. The weather has been damp or rainy all summer and all spring. Lister left the house this morning feeling dreadful; I hope he is not coming down with the flu.

Henrietta's school is out on the 5th. I believe now that I will be able to leave Washington around the 9th or 10th of the month. It takes me about ten days to pack, clean up the apartment, and to move.

Did you see an account of the new training school for pilots that will be opened at Maxwell Field, in Montgomery, in September? For the present the Tactical School will be abandoned and the field used to train pilots. This does not mean we are preparing for war, but we are getting prepared as quickly as possible to prevent a war. I expect to hear that England has been bombed within the next two weeks. War is so frightful!

I believe Congress will go ahead and adjourn around the 10th as scheduled, but we are apt to have to come back to Washington for an extra session in September.

Love, H.

P.S. There is an old Italian organ grinder playing outside our window. The children are wild about him and his monkey. The monkey is so cute, begging for pennies.

OCTOBER 31, 1941

This morning I received a notice that the President had appointed me to christen the "Battleship Alabama" this coming February. I am sure it will be the most thrilling occasion of my life. Really, it is a tribute to Lister, for his fine work and helpfulness.

Several days ago, Col. Edwin Watson, better known as "Pa" and who is one of FDR's closest friends, told Lister that when he had made the suggestion to the President that I should be chosen Sponsor of the Alabama, he exclaimed, "That is usually done by the Secretary of the Navy, but that is one appointment I am going to make myself."

DECEMBER 3, 1941

I am writing a column for the Sunday *Birmingham News*. Here is my first article:

Speaking of the future, in some ways it looks bright, but in others most depressing. From all I hear, the "Peace Emissary" from Tokyo— Saburo Kurusu—came to Washington just to stall for time. There are few people here who believe his intentions were ever honorable. If all negotiations fail between Tokyo and Washington then look for trouble P.D.Q.

If ever I am in need, I hope Mrs. Paul McNutt will sponsor "My Relief." Mrs. McNutt, who is a charming and capable woman, acted as Chairman of the "United China Relief" for Washington last week. The net proceeds from the benefit, a combination tea and bazaar, were well over six thousand dollars. The affair was held at the estate of

Mrs. Ann Archbald, a wealthy socialite. The ladies from the Chinese Legation, dressed in their charming native costumes, sold rice cakes throughout the afternoon. Enclosed in each crisp, flaky cookie was a slip of paper foretelling your fortune.

A Chinese dragon gaily danced about the lawn to the weird beating of a ceremonial drum in greeting Mrs. Roosevelt, who popped in and out again like a "Jack in the Box," as she does at all worthy benefits.

Mrs. Henry Haye, the wife of the Vichy Ambassador of France, surprised everyone by attending the fete.

For some reason, "Chinese Relief" seems to be more popular in Washington than British Relief. Not that the British aren't faring well, financially speaking—they have raised many times more money than the Chinese. The fact remains that the masses prefer to help the ever polite and humble Chinese. This feeling must be pretty general since the five-and-dime stores are flooded with Chinese wares, which indicates that sympathy for China has been sold to the American people.

Society in Washington is society with a purpose. Entertaining in Washington is so tied up with politics, that even the men in high positions scan the social column to see who is entertaining whom. I suppose it is the same in any national capitol. I have never known anything like the intrigue that has been going on in Washington.

Since Hitler chased royalty out of Europe, a number of these homeless refugees are living in the city. Among these settlers for the duration is the Archduke Otto of Hapsburg, pretender to the throne of Austria. Except for the Treaty of Versailles (and Adolph Hitler), he might now be Emperor of Austria, King of Hungary, Bohemia, Dalmatia, and Galicia. With dreams of such past glories, I can well understand why the romantic looking, twenty-eight-year-old "might have been," has sleepless nights wondering how he can recreate an Empire for himself. Although the Archduke lives in an unpretentious apartment at the Broadmoor, he has entertained extensively all the persons in the official set whom he feels could be useful in helping him make his dreams come true. As a beginning, his emissaries sought to lobby a bill through Congress, denying United States recognition of the Anschluss (the 1938 annexation of Austria into Germany, as orchestrated by the Nazis). This story leaked out the day before the Archduke's last party; as a consequence nary a Senator or Congressman appeared. The Congressional wives turned out in a good number, unaccompanied by their husbands. One Congressional wife remarked to me as we left the party together, "Fancy telling your grandchildren that you had tea with Royalty." These tales are going to be as numerous as the Lafayette Beds in America.

December 8, 1941
2540 Massachusetts Avenue, N.W.

Around four o'clock in the afternoon of December 7th our phone began to ring. The call came from a reporter who wanted to know if we had heard the news of the Japanese attack on Pearl Harbor. We were stunned.

As soon as Lister finished giving a statement to the press, he hung up the receiver. Then came a summons from the President, requesting Lister's immediate presence at the White House. Being that Lister is the Democratic Whip of the Senate and also a member of the Senate Military Committee, I don't imagine I will see much of him in the months to come.

The Wade Haislips live down the hall. The General and his lovely wife Alice were among the guests we had invited for a small dinner last night. Soon after Lister received his summons to the White House, "Ham" Haislip rapped on our door.

"I just want to ask if Lister would like to ride down to the White House with me?"

The two men left our apartment with heavy hearts.

General Haislip put Lister out at the Executive Office, then continued on to his own office, to await orders. Other guests called to ask if the dinner had been cancelled.

"If you had rather not come, I will certainly understand," I said. "Lister has gone to the White House and probably will not be returning until late, but Alice Haislip, Lister's brother Luther, and I are here and would be happy to see you."

The Drew Pearsons (he is a syndicated columnist for the *Post*), Dr. Lee Miller and his wife Hope (society editor of the *Washington Post*), Justice William Douglas and his wife Mildred, and the Buckley Griffins were among the guests. By the time Lister and General Haislip returned, most of the guests had left.

"Well, this is it," they both reported. "There will be a Joint Session of Congress tomorrow, and a formal Declaration of War."

We talked until quite late. Finally General Haislip said, "We are both hungry. Didn't you save us some of that ham?"

We fixed a plate of food for each of the men and served them some of my birthday cake with their coffee. Then Lister and I went to bed, but we were unable to sleep.

DECEMBER 13, 1941

Because of that "day which will live in infamy," Washington is filled with an unholy excitement. Excitement which, when it passes away, will leave in its place a realization of the long, hard days or years ahead.

Washington was appalled at the news of the attack by the Japanese. Yet knowing the methods employed throughout this war, of attacking and stunning the enemy while peace negotiations are in progress, it is amazing that America was taken completely off guard.

A few hours after news of the Japanese attack had circulated around Washington, hundreds of people filled with both anger and curiosity gathered on Massachusetts Avenue, in front of the artistic white and green mansion that is occupied by the Japanese Ambassador. I believe every camera owner in Washington was there, hoping to snap a picture of the Embassy and its occupants. Before the afternoon was over, the camera enthusiasts received their reward, for the Ambassador and Madam Nomura appeared for a moment in the front garden. They were a brave couple for they must have known that they would be greeted by boos and hisses.

No one in Washington believed the "peace emissary" ever had honorable intentions towards us. It seems that all Japanese diplomats in this country sold their automobiles two weeks ago.

A friend of mine, whose husband was once in the diplomatic service of France, told me that a Japanese member of the consular service from New York came by the preceding Wednesday to bid her goodbye. "Then this means war," she said. "Why can't our countries find a common meeting ground of understanding?" The Japanese flushed, and replied, "The United States will not recognize Japanese dominion of Manchukuo. The United States also passed the Japanese exclusion act." Under the existing law, the Japanese quota is one hundred persons a year.

Only those persons who were fortunate enough to obtain a pass to the Capitol on Monday morning were able to get within two blocks of the House of Representatives. Marines with fixed bayonets were stationed at intervals of fifteen feet. As you entered the Capitol grounds you were stopped every few feet to display your credentials. Uncle Sam, who was caught asleep at the switch on Sunday, was wide awake on Monday.

At a joint session of Congress, held only on momentous occasions, the Representatives file in and take their seats. (Members of Congress are already seated at the start of the meeting.) Next comes the Speaker of the House, who calls everyone to order. The Vice President then appears and takes a seat alongside of the Speaker on the rostrum. He is followed by the Senate Body. Next comes the Supreme Court, then the Cabinet and foreign Diplomats. When all are seated the Speaker announces, "The President of the United States."

In this case, cheers and more cheers, then Franklin D. Roosevelt ascended the ramp that is always provided for him. His face was tired and worn. His son James acted as his escort. When the President took the stand every man, woman, and child, every Republican, every isolationist, every Roosevelt hater, and every Democrat stood as united Americans and cheered for their President. It was amidst all this cheering and thunderous applause that I felt tears streaming down my face. A bit embarrassed, I turned away to discover that the lady by my side was weeping copiously, yet still applauding and smiling bravely. "Isn't it dreadful?" she asked. "I have three sons to go. What a dreary Christmas this will be for us."

On my way home, I circled around the Japanese Embassy. The crowds had dispersed. Only a number of photographers and newsmen and a sprinkling of policemen were still on guard, each waiting for the next move. I called to one of the reporters, "What's going on—are the Ambassador and his family about to leave America?" The reporter was most accommodating and told me all the news. "The Ambassador and his staff are waiting for the negotiations to go through before they can leave America. In the meantime, sixty American employees of the Embassy are imprisoned within. Under the law no one can go in or out of the Embassy until negotiations for the safe departure of the American Ambassador from Tokyo have been arranged. We have just sent in some food for the Americans."

"What is all the smoke out back?" I asked the reporter.

"Just more incriminating documents being destroyed," he replied. "They have been burning them since yesterday afternoon."

The apartment house in which we lived was flanked on one side by a vacant lot that was adjacent to the Japanese Embassy. I parked my car and stood for some moments in the vacant lot, which afforded an excellent view of the Embassy side yard. The Japanese Ambassador was playing a game of catch with one of the Embassy staff while he nonchalantly watched the clouds of smoke drifting heavenward. I couldn't help wondering if Ambassador Joseph Grew, our Ambassador to Japan, would be afforded such gentlemanly courtesies.

Cordell Hull, our universally revered Secretary of State, is perhaps the most miserable and depressed man in Washington today. After eight years of arbitration and tireless efforts for peace, he no doubt feels that his life's work has been futile. A most patient and honorable man, it is no wonder that he lost his temper when news reached him of the attack at Pearl Harbor. The Secretary, so the story goes, was cloistered with Kurusu and other representatives of the "Sun God," still discussing peace at the very time. From what I hear, the Tennessee mountain boy has a choice selection of "Sunday School words," which can outdo a Brooklyn sailor, and which he can use most effectively when thoroughly aroused. As the

"Peace Emissary" slunk from Mr. Hull's presence, he took with him a tongue-lashing he shall never forget.

Since war appears to be inevitable, as horrible as it seems, most people in authority seem to think that the attack of Pearl Harbor has united America in a way nothing else could have.

DECEMBER 20, 1941

It is good to feel that the Christmas spirit still prevails in Washington, despite the fact that America is at war.

Although the White House is blacked out, on Christmas Eve the President will follow his usual custom and light the lights on a giant Christmas tree that is planted on the White House lawn. As the tree is illuminated, thousands of men, women, and children from all walks of life will stand outside and serenade their President with Christmas carols. This year the carolers have chosen to sing "Joy to the World," "Oh Come All Ye Faithful," and "Silent Night." The program will begin just at dusk.

Let us all pray that when peace comes, it will bring with it a better understanding among the peoples of the earth. Had understanding and sympathy existed between nations, this war would never have begun.

An order for compulsory blackouts was issued yesterday to all occupants of apartment houses. With such a mad scramble for heavy black materials, the stores were soon sold out.

Mounted on the roofs of the White House, the Treasury, the Capitol, State, War, and Navy buildings are anti-aircraft guns awaiting their prey. Life in Washington goes on about the same, although a sort of hysteria still exists, especially among the children. Several mothers have told me that their children lie awake at night, fearful of an air raid. Realizing that many a child's Christmas might be marred by these fears, I have done what I could to reassure them. Yesterday, I spoke to a group of children ranging in ages from eight to twelve—kids who were eagerly looking forward to the annual visit of Santa Claus, that gray-bearded gentleman who is the most beloved of all characters. These children had just finished an air raid rehearsal at school, and I could see that the fear of an air raid was prevalent in their minds, so this is what I told them:

"I want all of you to be as happy as you can be this Christmas, and to forget that we are at war; but I do not want you to forget the 'Little Babe in the Manger,' Jesus Christ, whose birthday we celebrate. At Christmas time, Santa Claus so fills our minds and hearts that we are apt to forget the 'Little Lord Jesus.'

"If the war should be brought suddenly to you, and you are afraid, that is only natural. Do not cry aloud, for that confuses people around you. Lie very quietly, close your eyes and see if you can remember to repeat these words, 'Yea, though I walk through the Valley of the Shadow of Death, I will fear no evil, for thou are with me.' Try very hard to realize that if you believe in Jesus Christ, that He will protect you. The chances of your being hit in an air raid are very small. In London, where the British children have been bombed almost daily, only a relatively small percent of the people have been wounded. Many of those hurt are now recovered.

"If, however, you should be the victim of an air raid attack, do not be afraid, for on the other side of the door of life are many kind and loving people who will look after you.

"In a long war, many people are killed, but that need not distress you. These people might easily have been killed in an automobile wreck, died in a train wreck, of flu, or a thousand other causes. God promised Eternal Life to all of us who are good. The word *eternal* means *forever*. To compare Eternal Life to the longest life on earth is to compare one star to all the other stars in the Heavens, or one drop of water to all the water in the ocean. So you see, life at best is very short when compared to eternity. The thing that matters is how you spend those years, and if you have tried to leave the world a better place than you found it.

"I am telling you all these things because I do not want you to grow up with a black monster called 'Fear' always with you. If you can laugh and be gay, with the courage to take whatever comes, you need never be afraid."

There was a paragraph in the *Washington Post* on December 11 which I quote: "Naval officers declared here yesterday that they believe the successful Japanese air attack on the Americans and British fleets in the Pacific were launched by squadrons of kamikazes" who drove their planes straight into the warship targets. Upon meditation, this thought impressed itself indelibly on my mind. Such sacrifices, such acts of heroism must have been prompted by a force so great that it is difficult to defeat. Apparently the Japanese and German youths, as exhibited by their bravery, have little regard for life itself. Whether this intense patriotism is inspired or inbred I do not know. Statistics show, however, that more Japanese and German youths commit suicide than any other nationality. Embodied in the Japanese religion is a special proviso in the "hereafter," for anyone who commits "Hara-kiri." When a Japanese makes the supreme sacrifice for his country, an extra star is added to his "Crown of Glory." The only way in which we can combat such a force is to teach our children something of the Spirit of "Christ on Cavalry," who gave all, that others might have a better world in which to live.

JANUARY 1942

One day, I was in the lobby of the Shoreham Hotel waiting for a friend when along came Colonel B. whom we had known at Maxwell Field, Alabama. At that time, Britain was pleading for planes. The U.S. had steadfastly refused. I could not understand why, so I asked, "Bill, why don't we give Britain at least a few planes?"

He asked me, "Will you promise not to tell if I tell you the answer?" I promised. "The truth is we haven't got them to spare. Do you know how many air-worthy planes we have?" I shook my head. "At present we have one hundred fifty bombers, and we need every last one of them to train our own pilots."

The first mechanized cavalry was trained under Colonel Abner Chaffee at Fort Knox. A visiting group of Germans were so impressed by the mechanization of the cavalry that Hitler used the Colonel's ideas to build Germany's Panzer Divisions. Here in our country, the old time cavalry still clung to their horses just as the Admirals did the battleships.

JANUARY 18, 1942

Among the distinguished visitors to the Capital just now is our A.E.F. General John J. Pershing. General Pershing comes regularly to Walter Reed Hospital several times a year for a rest and check up. I am a great admirer of the General.

The newest and swankiest restaurant in Washington is called the "La-Salle de Bois." It is a French restaurant with a continental atmosphere, which serves excellent food. On Friday I lunched there with Mrs. Howard Davidson, who was evacuated from the Hawaiian Islands on one of the first ships to sail after the Japanese attack on Pearl Harbor. Her personal experiences were most interesting.

Last February, when she was in the States for a visit, I saw her one day, at a party. I have often thought of a remark she made to me at the time: "Coming to Washington has given me the jitters. You don't hear all this war talk out in Hawaii. I am going back out there where it is so peaceful." At the luncheon I couldn't help reminding her of her remarks. "Did you still have that same feeling of security up until the last?" I inquired.

Her reply was amazing. "We certainly did. We all thought that the worst thing that could happen to us was to be cut off by submarines from supplies from the United States. The only person who gave me any idea that something might happen was one friend, who advised the children and me to take tetanus serum against possible infection from shrapnel. We had just taken our tetanus shot on the Saturday before the War began."

I then asked her if she realized at that time the bombing began that it was the "real thing." She told us, "The attack began at exactly five minutes of eight. The noise sounded exactly like dynamiting, but it suddenly occurred to me that since it was Sunday, no dynamiting would be going on so I rushed outside to see what was up. Just two blocks away, planes were dropping bombs directly over the airfield. In great excitement I called to my husband, 'The Japs are here!' By this time planes were flying so low over the quarters that we had to duck and run for shelter, as the Japs had begun to machine gun the houses. My husband crawled along toward headquarters, dodging the machine gun fire as best he could. After ten minutes the raid was over, and the Japs had departed, only to return for a second time. By this time our men were in the air after them."

A few days after the attack, a convoy arrived at Pearl Harbor. My friend was among the persons ordered evacuated.

"On board ship," she said, "were many of the wounded, besides about a hundred women and children of the service group. The children and I decided to celebrate Christmas on the 21st in our cabin for we felt that we might not be living when Christmas Day came. The girls cut out a holly wreath from a piece of paper and pasted it around the porthole. Then they cut out paper chains of Christmas trees and Santa Clauses from red paper and strung them around the room. When they had finished, it really looked quite decorative. Someone took up a collection of objects to use as Christmas gifts for the wounded, to which I contributed my bedroom slippers. The morale was wonderful."

She told us that the laurels for heroism should go to a group of wives of enlisted men who volunteered to act as nurses for the wounded.

The last three days and nights of the trip were spent in life preservers. The ship finally docked on Christmas Eve, after zigzagging for seven days to dodge submarines. What a wonderful Christmas gift for anyone—to be given a chance at life again.

Among the passengers on this ship was an Argentine diplomat, returning from his post to his native country. Before the war was actually declared, he had been very pronounced in his pro-Japanese sentiments. On board ship he was more discreet.

I am leery of our Good Neighbor, Argentina. Wars are, for the most part, economic revolutions. For years the State Department has tried to induce this government to buy Argentine beef, but that comes in competition with our own cattle growers. Now for us to stand up and shout loud and lustily, "I'm your good friend! I'm your Good Neighbor!" and then do nothing about it fails to convince our good neighbors in South America. The time has passed when we can think only of ourselves and still live in a world at peace.

During the last two years, Washington has been South American minded—since the idea that they might be useful to us (yes, very useful) began to sink in. We now leave visiting cards on the South American diplomats, when we once only had time for the Europeans. We have changed the cocktail hour of four to six, to six to eight, to conform to a South American custom. We dance the rumba, and the conga, and applaud Carmen Miranda. We study Latin American foods and customs in our women's clubs, while the majority of our students are studying Spanish instead of French, but we do not buy Argentine beef. We used to slaughter pigs when we felt it expedient. Now we could buy Argentine beef and dump it in the ocean if necessary; it might even be cheap at that.

Rumors around Washington say that General George C. Marshall, Chief of Staff, has issued an order that no officer shall be seen at a cocktail bar, either public or private.

JANUARY 25, 1942

The minister of Czechoslovakia and Madam Hurban entertained at tea on Saturday, January 17th, in honor of the Minister of Foreign Affairs of Czechoslovakia, Mr. Jan Masaryk.

As I entered the hallway of the large and pretentious mansion, and stopped to check my wrap, I saw Mrs. Owen J. Roberts, [wife of an associate justice] of the Supreme Court. After we had exchanged greetings, I asked, "When is the Justice returning from Hawaii?"

"He is already back," was her reply.

"Of course, I am dying to hear his report," I said, half hoping she would comment.

Laughingly she said, "Just ask the taxi drivers. They will tell you." (The taxi drivers are the most talkative and know-all group in Washington.)

The drawing room and dining room of the Embassy are located on the second floor. As I ascended the stairway, I spoke to the Australian Minster and Mrs. Casey. The Caseys are a delightful couple, and far more like the average Americans than any of the other representatives from the British Commonwealth.

An announcer stood at the entrance of the drawing room, asking and announcing the names of the approaching guests to the host and hostess, and guest of honor. Just before I entered I heard him call out, "His

Excellency the Ambassador of Russia, and Madam Litvinoff," whereupon I was all eyes and ears, since I had not seen them before. Believe it or not, they had neither horns nor tails, but looked quite like ordinary folks here in America.

Later in the afternoon someone presented me to Madam Litvinoff. Being an English woman, she speaks perfect English, but slightly tinged with a foreign accent. She is a very plain though nice looking woman who still clings to the English custom of no makeup. Her costume couldn't have been simpler. Her dress was a tailored blue silk, with white collar and cuffs. She wore a light blue felt hat of the sports variety. Both Madam Litvinoff and the Ambassador have white hair and are in the stylish stout class.

I couldn't help telling her how proud we all are of the wonderful success of the Russian Army against Hitler's legions. She seemed quite pleased. Altogether, I found her a most agreeable person.

Speaking of Russian successes, an Army man told me several days ago not to be overconfident about them; that he thinks part of the so-called German crackup is just another Hitler trick to delude us into believing "all is well."

Among other guests of the Czechoslovakian Minister and his wife that afternoon were most of the Supreme Court, a smattering of our Army and Navy, a representative group from both Houses of Congress, a group of Washingtonians, the Washington Press, and all of our present day allies, minus the British. Even the Poles (who grabbed a portion of Czechoslovakia) were present—but the British were conspicuous by their absence. I don't think the Czechs can ever forget Mr. Neville Chamberlain and the Munich Agreement (which appeased Hitler).

As I was leaving the tea, I saw Madam Bruggman (the wife of the Swiss Minister) and the sister of the Vice President just arriving. The Swiss Minister had bestowed upon the VP the handling of all German affairs in this country. I don't believe he was keen on the job, but look at Switzerland's position today. Would he have a chance?

Saturday seemed to be Diplomatic Day. The Turkish Ambassador and Madam Ertegun celebrated their Silver Anniversary with a large reception. The Turks at the present time are being wooed by all nationalities as possible allies. I believe they would prefer to line up with us, if they are allowed to choose for themselves. When Turkey was modernized some fifteen years ago, the Ambassador took a new name. *Ertegun* means "The Day After."

The hoarders in Washington had a field day this last week. There was a run at all the grocery stores on staple foods that practically stripped the shelves of flour, sugar, lard, canned goods, soaps, and toilet tissue. One woman complained because she could buy no sugar, but remarked as she left the store, "Oh well, I have a hundred and fifty pounds on hand."

Cases of canned goods and other stock disappeared into waiting limousines. The rich, however, were not the only hoarders. Housewives from all walks of life carried away as much as they could load into their automobiles. The sight made me sick at heart, and I was tempted to yell out after them, "Slackers! Fifth Columnists! Where is your patriotism? Why haven't you thought of your neighbor? Don't you know that you are creating a panic?"

Of course, we will be driven to food rationing right away, if people have no more foresight than this.

I asked the grocery clerk if he couldn't do something to stop this wholesale buying, and limit the number of purchases of a given article to a customer. He told me that something would have to be done since transportation facilities are slowed up by this emergency and it would be weeks before he could replace his stock.

Unless measures are taken immediately, those who are too poor or too patriotic to buy up foodstuffs will go hungry in the nation's Capital. This is no way to win a war. We must all fight together.

FEBRUARY 1942

The next day, Mrs. Roosevelt visited the Senate Ladies Red Cross meeting, to have lunch with us. Since the war began we have met twice a week to roll bandages and to sew for the Red Cross. Each member brings her own sandwich, while some of the ladies make coffee on a hot plate. Mrs. R. even offered to bring her own sandwich, but we felt we should supply it for her.

After we had finished luncheon, Mrs. Roosevelt arose and said, "Ladies, I have not prepared a speech for you this morning. It occurred to me that there might be many things troubling you at this time, which you would like to discuss. Are there any questions you would like to ask?"

There was dead silence. No one arose to ask a question. After the passage of some minutes, it seemed to me that someone ought to start the ball rolling, so I arose and addressed the First Lady. "Mrs. Roosevelt, I have been very much disturbed by the hoarding I have seen going on in Washington. What do you think we can do about it?"

Mrs. Roosevelt gulped and sputtered and looked thoroughly confused. Everybody began to snicker. By this time, I was confused too. Then one of my friends, who understands my Southern accent, arose and said, "Mrs. Roosevelt, Mrs. Hill did not mean what you think she did, that is just her Southern accent. She meant H-O-A-R-D-I-N-G not W-H-O-R-I-N-G!"

Mrs. R. gathered her composure. "There is plenty of food in this country and no shortages, but if hoarding continues, of course we will be forced to have rationing just as Britain does."

I am now Secretary of the Senate Ladies Red Cross Unit, but I did not record this little incident.

Incidentally, I have been instrumental in changing the name of our group from the Senate Ladies Luncheon Club to the Senate Ladies Red Cross Unit. I think it is more in keeping with the work we are doing.

Shantytown is again rising in Washington, just as it did in the last war. Every morning when I drive Lister to the Capitol, a new temporary war building has been started. The first morning there is a pile of lumber, the next a building; the third day it has been stuccoed, and the fourth it is about ready to turn over to the defense workers. It took twenty-five years to dispose of the last crop of shanties, and now a new crop has sprung up.

Although little is said about them, there are definite signs of air raid shelters being built in Washington. Around the White House, at intervals of twenty feet, are little sentinel houses that have been painted a dark green, each occupied by a soldier with a fixed bayonet. How different from the days of the two thousand daily tourists at the White House, and the five thousand children rolling Easter eggs on the lawn, with the Marine Band playing. Maybe that is what we are fighting for anyway.

FEBRUARY 1, 1942

The Alabama State Society of Washington held its annual reception in honor of their Congressional Delegation on January 24th, in the main ballroom of the Willard Hotel. This year's President, Congressman Pete Jarman, who is putting lots of pep into the Society, headed the receiving line, accompanied by his attractive wife, Beryl Bricken Jarman, who wore a chic black lace dinner dress. Mrs. Jarman has been her husband's secretary ever since he was elected to Congress and is one of the hardest working women in Washington.

Senator and Mrs. John Bankhead were next in line, the latter wearing a copper-colored evening gown that blended beautifully with her Titian hair. We hope that Mrs. Bankhead will remain in Washington for a spell, but just as soon as she hears that the daffodils are blooming in her garden in Jasper, I'm afraid she will be off again for Alabama.

Lister and I stood next beside the Bankheads. I wore a chiffon dress of a lovely shade of coral.

The entire Alabama delegation and their wives were present with only two exceptions: Congressman Sam Hobbs, who was out of town, and Mrs. Joe Starnes, who hasn't put in an appearance as yet this winter. I understand that Joe has at last located an apartment for his family and is expecting them on February 1st.

The most unusual coiffure among the ladies belongs to Mrs. George Grant, wife of the Representative from Union Springs. Her hair, which is a bright golden yellow and almost waist length, is worn straight back in a bun, without a single crinkle, which makes her distinctive in this age of permanent waves. The Grants are the proud parents of a four-month old son.

We were all delighted to see Mrs. Sam Hobbs at the Ball, in spite of the fact that her husband was in Alabama. This was one of Sarah Ellen's first appearances since she was so badly injured in an automobile wreck last July near Atlanta.

Frank Boykin, a Congressman from Mobile, Alabama, with his sweet wife Ocello on his arm, looked as proud as a peacock as he strutted in the grand march. Patriotism has hit the Boykin family with a bang. Their two oldest sons volunteered for service in the Air Corps recently, and it took much persuasion to keep their last son, not yet eighteen, from joining with his brothers.

Among the guests present at the Society Saturday night were Colonel and Mrs. Marion Rushton and their attractive young daughter, Camilla, of Montgomery. Colonel Rushton, who is Alabama's Democratic National Committeeman and is also Governor Frank Dixon's Montgomery County campaign manager, has recently been assigned to duty in the Judge Advocate General's Office in Washington.

Colonel "Tackey" Gayle, Montgomery's City Commissioner, who was on hand, spent the evening answering inquiries about the condition of his uncle, governor Bibb Graves, who underwent an operation at Johns Hopkins Hospital in Baltimore on Friday. From all reports the Governor is "keeping on keeping on."

Alabama's representative on the ICC, Hayden Aldridge and Mrs. Aldridge, were seen chatting with Colonel and Mrs. Allen Crenshaw of Andalusia.

There are now about three thousand Alabamians living in Washington. They were not all present at the Ball on Saturday night, but they were there in sufficient numbers to make one feel that it was "Old Home Week" in the Nation's Capital.

In baseball three strikes are out, but it took Iola (Mrs. Henry) Wallace nine strikes to christen the Transatlantic plane *Excalibur* at Stratford, Connecticut, recently. With each blow there were gales of laughter, but that did not shake the determination of our Vice President's wife. Mrs. Wallace explained to friends afterwards, "The plane was too soft and I made a lovely dent in it. I was never so grateful to anyone in my life as to the man who finally placed an iron pipe on the nose of the plane."

On January 26th, General Douglas MacArthur celebrated his sixty-second birthday. Members of both Houses of Congress at a joint session arose amidst tumultuous cheers to pay tribute to this gallant soldier on his birthday. Military experts who know something of the caliber of the man say that he will never surrender, but will fight to the last man.

Several days ago Mrs. Lionel Atwell attended a small luncheon at the home of a friend. Somehow the conversation got around to her former husband, General MacArthur. "He certainly seems to be a brave man," one of the guests said. With a twinkle in her eye, Louise Atwell (who was MacArthur's first wife) replied, "He proved that when he married me."

Another great American celebrated his birthday this week—our President Franklin D. Roosevelt. Washington is flooded with movie stars who came here to attend the numerous Birthday Balls, which were held at all of the leading hotels on Friday night.

On Thursday Mrs. Alben Barkley, Mrs. Walter George, and Mrs. Robert LaFollette honored these movie stars with a reception at the Willard Hotel. This was really a gala occasion. Movie stars affect me strangely. I have the feeling that they are not quite human—as if an old family portrait that I had looked at for years suddenly came to life and, stepping down from its frame, began speaking to me. When I was engaged in conversation with Robert Montgomery I had a wild desire to stick a pin in him to see if he would squeal—but Bob, being quite human, might have objected. Lieutenant Montgomery, who is now on duty in Washington, was quite handsome, dressed in his "Navy Blues." The last I saw of him, he was completely surrounded by ladies, both young and old.

Speaking of being surrounded, the glamorous Dorothy Lamour put all the local beauties in the shade. The men were all swarming to get a sight of her.

Gene Autry, Mickey Rooney, and Edward Arnold all came in for their share of attention; in fact, this was one time our local celebrities had to take a back seat, but they all seemed to enjoy it.

FEBRUARY 8, 1942

All of Washington celebrated the birthday of President Roosevelt last week in a variety of ways.

Preceding the Birthday Balls, a banquet was held at the Willard Hotel, which was attended by a host of movie stars, diplomats, high-ranking service officers, members of Congress, and residentials. About five hundred guests gathered in the flag-festooned main ballroom of the Willard where the tables were arranged.

Scattered about in the crowd were the chief of Staff and Mrs. George C. Marshall; the Chief of Naval Operations and Mrs. Harold R. Stark; Mr. and Mrs. Edward Stettinius; Lord and Lady Halifax (British Ambassador); the Soviet Ambassador and Madam Litvinoff; Jesse Jones (the Secretary of Commerce) and Mrs. Jessie Jones; the Chinese Ambassador Dr. Hu Shi (pronounced *Hugh She*); Archduke Otto of Austria; and scores of others.

Directly behind me sat Mrs. Patrick Hurley whose husband was this week appointed to serve as our first Minister to New Zealand. General Hurley had already arrived at his destination before the announcement of his appointment was made. Mrs. Hurley and her two unmarried daughters have remained in Washington for the "duration."

Mrs. Evelyn Walsh McLean may be down but she is never out. After selling her estate "Friendship" to the Government for a defense housing project, she purchased another mansion on "R" Street. As a departure from her usual custom of entertaining numerous guests at the "Gold Plate Breakfast" (twenty dollars a plate) held at the Carlton Hotel each year after the last strains of the President's Birthday Balls have died away, Mrs. McLean contented herself this year with a "house warming" party in her new home, before the various balls began.

I noticed on her guest list the following celebrities: Justice and Mrs. Stanley Reed, Justice and Mrs. William O. Douglas, the Swiss Minister and Madam Charles Bruggman (sister of Henry Wallace), the Summer Welles (our Assistant Secretary of State, who has just returned from Rio and the Pan American Conference), New Jersey's Governor and Mrs. Charles A. Edison (son of Thomas A. Edison), J. Edgar Hoover (FBI),

Mr. and Mrs. Leon Henderson (Price-fixing), Fulton and Lady Lewis (Radio Commentator), and Mr. and Mrs. John L. Lewis (CIO). The other hundred guests were just Senators and Congressmen and Washington socialites.

Down in the Hunt Country, Mr. Walter P. Chrysler gave the use of his home in Warrenton, which was formerly the North Wales Country Club for a Birthday Ball. A large number of Washington debutantes drove the forty miles to attend the festivities there. The Club was in complete blackout and was stocked with food against a possible air raid.

Perhaps the gayest party of all was held at the Lincoln Colonnade, where Louise Beavers acted as toastmistress. From all accounts from our cook, it was quite a party.

After the ball is over—and the stars have departed our town, I am going to be impolite enough to talk behind their backs. They were a grand crowd, always eager to do their part in helping any just cause, but if you have a favorite glamour girl or a secret sorrow in the movies, remember the old adage "distance lends enchantment." Few of them are ever as beautiful or charming as they appear on the screen. Among the men who were here last week, Lieutenant James Stewart, Gene Raymond, and Robert Montgomery were the most attractive. The two best-looking actresses were young Pat Morrison and Brenda Frazer.

Former Congressman and Mrs. Miles C. Allgood of the Seventh Alabama District celebrated their twenty-fifth wedding anniversary last Sunday by entertaining at a reception in their Virginia home. The secret was so well guarded by the host and hostess that most of the guests were unaware this was a special occasion until they spied the large and beautiful wedding cake in the center of the dining room table. Mrs. Allgood looked particularly lovely on Sunday, and their many friends congratulated Miles for having won so sweet and gentle a wife.

Several years ago the Allgoods purchased an old farmhouse near both Mount Vernon and Woodlawn. Many hours of labor have gone into the reclaiming of this attractive homestead since Miles decided to become a gentleman farmer. Now they are fearful that they will have to move to St. Louis with his division of the Agricultural Department, which is scheduled to leave Washington during this emergency. The party on Sunday, we all regretted to hear, may have been a farewell to the Allgoods.

Justice Jimmie Byrnes, the latest addition to the Supreme Court, is wondering if his wire-haired terrier will next week conform to "War Time," or if he will have to purchase himself an alarm clock. For years the Justice's pet has gently tapped him with his paw on the abdomen at seven-fifteen each morning; a reminder that it was time to arise.

Speaking of dogs, the William O. Douglas's, the Bob Jacksons, and the Hugo Blacks all have dogs. The Douglas's pet is an English Spaniel; the Blacks have a West Highland Terrier named Peppermint (looks like a Scottie with stiff white hair similar to a wire-haired terrier); and I think someone told me that the Jacksons had a coach dog, a sporty black-spotted animal.

Incidentally the Jacksons have purchased a lovely country place near McLean, Virginia, about fifteen miles from Washington. The Blacks live near the heart of historic Alexandria in a charming old brick house that was built in seventeen-something. (After the death of Justice Jackson, Mrs. Jackson sold her home "Hickory Hill" in Langley, Virginia, to Senator and Mrs. John F. Kennedy. A short while later the Kennedys sold this house to his brother Bob and his nine children.) The Byrnes still keep their apartment at the Shoreham Hotel and their home in South Carolina.

Mrs. Roosevelt is wearing black cotton stockings everywhere these days. It looks as if the cotton farmer at last has a lucky break. Some of the new suntan shades are quite lovely and I dare say will outlast black hose ten to one.

Get your bicycle ready. They are quite fashionable now. It looks as if we were going back to ye good ol' days of "Daisy, Daisy, Give Me Your Promise True"—and a bicycle built for two.

The Lucky USS Alabama

The christening of the U.S.S. *Alabama* at the Portsmouth, Virginia, Navy Yard on last Monday, February 16th, was a day which will long live in the memory of all those who were present to witness the ceremonies for which I acted as a sponsor.

To those who have never seen the launching of a great ship, it is difficult to describe the emotional experience. Picture, if you can, a more dramatic setting—the whole world at war; America fighting for existence; flags flying; the band playing; thousands of people standing in a drizzling rain; workmen hanging from steel rafters; newsreels grinding; cameras clicking; and planes flying overhead for our protection. With all of this there is a tenseness that comes from anticipation of a great moment, when a magnificent spirit is released.

I did not know until I witnessed the birth of the mighty battleship *Alabama* that ships had souls and were personalities, nor did I know that sponsors and Secretaries of the Navies and "old sea dogs" wept from the sheer majesty and import of such an occasion.

Tremendously impressive were the speeches of the Secretary of the Navy, Frank Knox, and of the Governor of Alabama, Frank Dixon. Secretary Knox told a cheering throng that the *Alabama* is one of the ships that will bring us victory, while Governor Dixon said, "The *Alabama* carries the hearts and hopes of all free men and women on earth today." I was proud of the speech which Governor Dixon made. It could not have been more dignified nor appropriate.

"And see she stirs,
She starts, she moves,
She seems to feel
The thrill of life along her keel."
—*Excerpt from Longfellow's "The Launching of a Ship"*

There must have been an expression of surprise on my face as when I smashed the bottle of champagne against the hull I alone seemingly sent the *Alabama* down the Elizabeth River. Later I found out that the electrical signals had failed to work and the only warning I had that the great ship was about to slide down the ways was given by the aide who stood beside me with his hand on the ship and yelled, "Hit her now! She is moving!" I doubt if a second blow would have been possible, had the first failed.

There is an old superstition among sailors that if the bottle of champagne fails to break and a ship goes un-christened, it is an ill omen, and the ship is doomed from the start.

I can still hear the cheering, the whistles blowing, and the band playing "The Star Spangled Banner" and I shall always remember the prayer in my heart for the *Alabama*.

To add a humorous note to a most solemn occasion, I shall never forget the workman who stood beneath the Sponsor's platform with a tin box in his hand trying to catch a few drops of champagne as the bottle crashed.

A ship launching seems comparatively simple to a layman, but I learned while at Portsmouth that it took two thousand men working all night long on Sunday night to get the *Alabama* in readiness to slide down the ways. Each peg which held her "on her way" had to be removed at a specific time, each inch of rail had to receive a certain amount of grease. The details of a launching are both intricate and tedious, requiring expert engineering skill.

At one time on Sunday night, the Commanding Officer thought that the christening would have to be postponed. The tide was wrong, the wind was wrong, and the predictions were for rain. What if the mighty ship failed to move? It was not until eleven o'clock that a decision was reached to "go ahead."

Much has been written about ship christenings, of speakers, of sponsors, and of presents. The other side of the picture has not been shown. The christening of a ship is also a celebration for the workmen who by their toil and sweat have created a masterpiece and are proud to display their handiwork. That these men might have a part in the christening ceremonies, the names of all the young girls whose fathers had a part in the construction of the *Alabama* were placed in a hat and drawn. The fortunate young lady who had her name drawn was then chosen as flower girl to the Sponsor. Lovely little Audrey Noble, the daughter of one of the master foremen, attended me and presented me with a large bouquet of American Beauty roses.

The Maid of Honor, Julia Ann Sparkman, the daughter of Congressman and Mrs. Sparkman, was personally chosen by me as my attendant—she quite captivated all the young Ensigns with her dimples and large dark eyes.

After the ceremonies we drove to the reception. Here, I got my first good look at the gift which was first presented to me during the exercises—a large and handsome silver bowl engraved in the bottom: "U.S.S. *Alabama*—February 16, 1942—Portsmouth, Virginia—Henrietta Hill, Sponsor." Upon inquiry I was told that the gift was presented by the workmen who built the *Alabama*, and purchased with a fund collected by them. The donations for this fund ranged from one to ten cents, and so that is what I meant when I said, "I shall always treasure this beautiful gift since it comes to me from every one connected with the construction of the *Alabama*."

I also received a mahogany box containing the remnants of the bottle used in the christening. This bottle was encased in a steel mesh case to prevent me from cutting my hand. This case had received such a hard blow that it was badly dented, and broken in places. I was so afraid I would not break the bottle on the first go round that "I gave it all I had!"

There was a receiving line at the luncheon headed by Admiral Gygax, the Commandant of the Navy Yard, who introduced the guests to me.

I in turn presented them to the Maid of Honor. Next stood the Flower Girl, the Secretary of the Navy, Frank Knox, the Governor of Virginia and Mrs. Darden, and the Governor of Alabama and Mrs. Dixon.

I wore a "christening robe," a black silk "Hattie Carnegie" dress and hat. The neckline was a V shape, the skirt of the new Harem style, and the sleeves were of three-quarter length. The belt on the dress was of tobacco brown suede, held together with a gold dagger. My hat was of the calot type, worn so often by the Duchess of Windsor. A corsage of orchids and the large armful of roses that I held all during the reception brightened the costume.

Julia Ann Sparkman's costume was of French blue, with a matching hat. Her corsage was of gardenias. Audrey Noble wore a cream-colored silk dress with a luggage tan hat, tied under her chin with ribbons. Her flowers were of Sweetheart roses and forget-me-nots.

Alabama's First Lady, Mrs. Frank Dixon, chose for her costume an "Eisenberg" model gray-plaid woolen suit, the blouse of which was fashioned from pearl gray satin on which were sewed large rhinestone buttons. Her hat was a large felt in matching tones and her flowers were yellow orchids.

At the luncheon, a long table was placed in the center of the room. Directly behind the table, one of the Navy gobs had painted a replica of the U.S.S. *Alabama* as she will look upon completion. At the Sponsor's table sat the two Governors and their wives, Admiral Gygax and Mrs. Gygax, Justice and Mrs. Hugo Black, Lister and our young daughter Henrietta, Congressman and Mrs. John Sparkman, the Maid of Honor, Mr. and Mrs. Noble and Audrey Noble.

The Governor's staff was seated at a table directly opposite the Sponsor's table. There were six Mayors and their wives present, including the Mayor of Birmingham and Mrs. Cooper Green, the Mayor of Bessemer and Mrs. Jap Bryant and their daughter, Mayor and Mrs. Bloom of Homewood, Mayor and Mrs. W.S. Coleman of Anniston, Mayor Herbert Meighan of Gadsden and Mayor and Mrs. Lucien Burns of Selma.

I would judge that about one hundred persons from Alabama attended. The majority of those present consisted of the Naval Officers stationed at the Portsmouth Navy Yard and their wives. As Admiral Gygax said, "We were sorry not to have been able to issue more invitations to Alabamians but these are war times, and precautions are absolutely necessary."

MARCH 7, 1945

Dearest Mama,

I am sorry to have waited so long to answer your letter, but I have been very busy. Have just finished writing ten thank-you notes to people who have given money or donated books for the Battleship *Alabama*. The drive closed yesterday and we sent five hundred books to the ship.

Among the autographed books, which I received from the authors, were Sumner Wells' *Time for Decision*, Henry Wallace's *Democracy Reborn*, Joseph Grew's *Ten Years in Japan*, Joe Davies' *Mission to Moscow*, Katherine Bowen's *Yankee from Olympus*, Archibald MacLeish's *A Time to Act*, Jospehus Daniels' *Wilson Era*, Mrs. Ray Clapper's *Watching the World*, Vera Bloom's *There Is No Place Like Washington*, and Mrs. Frances Parkinson Keyes new novel (I have forgotten the title). Then I collected sixty dollars and purchased all of the books on *The New York Times* best-seller list. I feel that I have done a good job for my ship. I believe I wrote you that Dr. Leslie Glenn, who is the Minister of St. Johns Church here in Washington, is the Chaplain of the *Alabama*. Dr. Glenn wrote asking me to try to send some books to the ship as they had so few in the ship's library. Thank you for the books you sent.

Love, H.

NAVY RELIEF SOCIETY
NAVY DEPARTMENT
WASHINGTON D.C.

MARCH 9, 1949

My Dear Senator Hill,

In a conversation with Representative Noble Gregory the other day we were discussing little known episodes of Navy ships. I told him the history of the enclosed picture. He said he knew you and Mrs. Hill quite well and he felt sure that you would be interested in having a copy of it.

Its history is as follows. When I took command of the *Alabama* in July of 1944, just prior to the Polius, Philippine, Okinawa, and Formosa strikes, I had some pictures taken to send home to my wife and mother. Quite inadvertently, Mrs. Hill's picture was included in this one.

It is interesting, I think that when the ship was stripped for action, all potential hazards, and flying bric-a-brac, pictures, etc. were removed and stored away. As the Sponsor of the ship, Mrs. Hill's picture was not removed. It was, however, the only one left and was in the Captain's cabin as you see. It may be superstition but at any rate the ship was not hit by the Japs or for that matter anybody else during the war. You can call it what you want to, but it worked.

I told my ship yeoman to make these pictures up for Mrs. Murphy. When he came to this one, he brought it back—with some advice. He said in effect, this is a picture of a very attractive lady; maybe you better put a word of explanation to your wife. I don't see her picture anywhere.

I did just that and we're living happily ever after.

The above is a true story. If it is of any interest to you or to Mrs. Hill, I am happy to send you the picture.

Sincerely yours,
V.R. Murphy
Vice Admiral, U.S. Navy (Retired)

There was never a night when I went to bed during the war that I did not pray for the protection of the *Alabama*. The ship, as Admiral Murphy testifies, was not harmed in battle. She won nine battle stars in action. Admiral John Franklin Shafroth was Commander of Battleship Squadron 2, which was part of the task force operating outside of Tokyo Bay in a full readiness state at the time of the Japanese surrender. He was called in to Tokyo Bay to witness the surrender, and after it was concluded orders were sent to the ships of Battleship Squadron 2, and it led the column of the vessels of Squadron 2 in Tokyo Bay a day or so after the surrender.

The *Alabama*, like so many of her sister ships, was put in mothballs on the West Coast. When it was announced that she was to be scrapped, the citizens of Alabama raised the money to purchase her.

The prayer that I uttered the day the ship slid down the ways was, "Oh Lord, bring her safely home again." I am sure there were many prayers said for her, both at the christening and there afterwards.

In 1965 the ship was towed from Seattle to Mobile Bay where it is now a memorial to Alabama's heroes of World War II. Today, it ranks third as a tourist attraction in the state, 600,000 people having visited the *Alabama* this past year.

The War Years

FEBRUARY 24, 1942

Washington is very exciting now, though terribly overcrowded with so many defense workers, patriots, and "dollar a year" men (volunteers, usually industrialists, working in Washington for token pay). Several days ago I went to a garage to have a smashed fender repaired and had to wait three days before I could get the job done the garage manager told me that 45,000 new people had come to Washington during the past few months. The garage had more business than they could do.

It is almost impossible to get a hotel room or a place to live. The housing authorities look for an acute shortage by fall. There is a wonderful story going the rounds in Washington about the housing shortage. A drowning man in the Potomac River screamed, "Help, help." A passerby seeing the man yelled back, "What's your name?" Gulping, the man yelled back, "Jones." When the victim in the river came up the second time, the man on the bank called to him, "What's your address? As the drowning man went down the third time he answered in desperation, "1212 Que Street, N.W.," whereupon the man on the bank jumped into a taxi and hurried to the address given him by the deceased. "I want to rent Mr. Jones' apartment," he said breathlessly. "Sorry," replied the landlord, "I have already rented it to the man who pushed him in." (The above story was reported by Hope Riding Miller in the *Washington Post*.)

In spite of the existing law that was supposed to freeze rentals in the District of Columbia, property owners are in many cases ejecting their tenants when their leases expire, under the guise of reclaiming their property for their own personal use, and then renting to more prosperous persons for double the price. The salaried families are caught in the middle of a sad predicament. For a Member of Congress who makes $835 per month (less income tax), such rentals, plus the rising costs of living, not to mention campaign expenses, will be prohibitive. Many a Congressional family will be forced to return to their native states, leaving their husbands to abide in the boarding houses on Capitol Hill.

The Trubee Davidsons (former Assistant Secretary of War under Hoover) leased a house on Observatory Circle recently. The house rented for $450 per month on the morning before the Davidsons moved in, but jumped to $650 the afternoon of the same day when the Davidsons took possession.

The recently married Jock Whitneys have likewise had rental troubles. Mrs. Whitney is the former Betsy Cushing Roosevelt (ex-wife of James Roosevelt). Before Jock Whitney knew that he would take unto himself a wife, he rented a house in the vicinity of the British Embassy for the fabulous sum of $650 per month. Written in his lease was a provision that stated "No Children." Try as he did, he could not convince his landlord that Betsy's two children were not objectionable, so he rented the Cary Grayson house at an equally costly rental to house his newly acquired family.

Several friends who lived here during the First World War have told me that Congress never did adjourn all during that time. They are quite certain that Congress will stay in continuous session during this war. I have been trying to persuade Lister to buy a small house in Spring Valley. We have to pay three thousand dollars a year for this apartment and it is so much money down the drain. More important still, we don't know when we might find ourselves on the street. There are rumors that the rent is due for an increase before rent control goes into effect. I don't much mind having the children cooped up in an apartment during the winter months, but if we have to stay here in summer it isn't fair to them. Then there is the question of our dog Champ; so many apartments refuse to take dogs. Many of the apartment buildings take the other attitude and display signs: "One well behaved dog allowed, no children." Most of them state "No Children or Dogs."

During my first sixteen years in Washington we moved thirty-two times—twice each year. When war came we were forced to buy a house to secure a place to live, because we could not afford Washington's high rentals on a yearly basis.

I RAN INTO SENATOR Walter George in the Capitol yesterday and asked him if his wife Lucy was going to the luncheon in the Speakers Dining Room. Whereupon he replied, "Did anyone ask her? If so, she will be there." Senator George rarely goes out socially, but Lucy loves people and is invited out a lot. Mary Jim Smathers (wife of Senator Jim Smathers of New Jersey) whom I was with yesterday at the Capitol, told me that Miss Lucy had taken up piano lessons again after twenty years, and that Senator Glass, who has an apartment under the George's at the Mayflower Hotel, has threatened to move unless Lucy soon learns the "Happy Farmer."

Everybody loves "Miss Lucy." If you see her at a party surrounded by a group of friends, she is apt to be saying, "Have you heard this one?" "Miss Lucy" likes to tell slightly off-color stories.

Rather late in life, "Miss Lucy" has suddenly developed a desire to have her own bank account—something she had never experienced. As Lucy argued with the erudite Senator, she firmly declared, "Now, Mr. George [she always addressed him formally], I am going to have my own bank account, even if I have to get a job." The Senator reluctantly agreed, but there was one stipulation. The Senator insisted that his wife keep a record of her expenditures. At the end of the first month, Senator George demanded a look at Lucy's account. During the inspection, he noted several entries, each labeled D.I.I.K. Puzzled, he inquired, "Lucy, what is this item—D.I.I.K.?"

Her reply was typical: "Darned If I Know."

AUGUST 18, 1938

During the 1938 campaign for reelection of the Georgia Democratic Congressional Delegation to the Congress, Franklin D. Roosevelt spoke in Barnesville, Georgia, Seated beside the President on the platform, Senator George waited his time to speak. Near the end of his oration, the President asked the audience to purge the veteran Senator George from the U.S. Senate due to his too conservative voting record and his opposition to the Supreme Court Packing plan bill. When the President concluded, Walter George walked to the front of the platform and in a clear, firm voice replied, "Mr. President, I accept the challenge." Senator George won reelection to the Senate easily.

One day, the Women's Director for the reelection of Senator George approached Mrs. George. "Mrs. George," she said, "you have got to attend some of the ladies luncheons. They are given for you. You won't have to make a speech, just stand up and let them see you and say 'I am so glad to be here' and then sit down." Lucy promised to give it a try.

The ladies of Gainesville, Georgia, who were honoring Mrs. George with a luncheon, were eagerly awaiting an introduction to the candidate's wife. With trembling legs and pounding heart, Miss Lucy arose. "I am so happy to be in Barnesville today." The crowds roared with laughter. Miss Lucy turned to the Women's Director, saying, "You see? I told you I could not make a speech." The lady seated next to Mrs. George whispered, "Honey, you are in Gainesville today. Barnesville was yesterday."

SOME FOLKS ARE NATURALLY "agin"—like the old man who rose up in a political meeting and said, "I don't know what it is, but I'm agin it."

As has been customary for many years, on February 22, Washington's Farewell Address was read in the Senate. This year Senator Theodore Green of Maine was chosen to read the Address. A constituent of the Senator's wrote him, protesting: "You are an old fogie. Why dig up ancient documents in times like these? I object to your taking up the Senate's time to read Washington's Farewell Address."

MARCH 1, 1942

Washington right now is like a huge jigsaw puzzle that has been carelessly dumped upon the floor. Only a "master mind" could solve this giant puzzle and fit these muddled pieces into a harmonious picture.

Society moves on at a rapid pace, as if it feared it was having its last fling. London and Paris were much the same in the days of that "phony war" before the grimness of total war set in.

Sniped at, but recuperating, is Congress, who first passed, then repealed, the misnamed "Pension Bill," which was, in truth, an extension of Social Security to Members of Congress. Said one Member, "I feel we should be allowed the privileges of Social Security by paying in a portion of our salaries each month, as prescribed by the Bill, but the country has expressed its displeasure over the measure, and it is the desire of Congress to keep the complete confidence and faith of all our people at this time."

In connection with the repealed "Congressional Pension Bill," let me say that I have never known a Member of the Congress who did not have enough outside means when he was elected to leave Washington with any money in his pockets. The high cost of campaigns, the high cost of living in a great city, and a thousand other things makes poor men of most of these public servants. Many of them leave their families destitute.

When Joe Robinson, once the Democratic Leader of the Senate, died, his wife (who was then well in her fifties) took a job as postmistress in her hometown in Arkansas. Up until her retirement last year, when she retired, Mrs. William J. Harris (the white-haired widow of Sen. Harris of Georgia, and a daughter of General Joe Wheeler of Alabama) also worked as a postal clerk, selling stamps to Senators in the Capitol. There have been many others who have proudly starved, forgotten by the public.

To give you a few tidbits with the demitasse: I am afraid that the Democrats have permanently lost John L. Lewis. Last week Lewis celebrated his birthday jointly with Princess Alice Roosevelt Longworth. The party was held in the Alexandria home of the Lewises. During the afternoon a large birthday cake bearing two candles, one for each of the "luminaries," was brought in to the guests of honor. I was told that Princess Alice entertained for Mr. Lewis at a similar party last year, so when the birth date rolled around again, Mr. Lewis returned the compliment.

The night Singapore fell, Lord and Lady Halifax were entertaining a few friends at the British Embassy. When news was brought to the Ambassador that Singapore had finally been lost, he is said to have remarked, "Oh really—but we will get it back again." My informer told me she felt like saying, "D— the complacency of the British!"

Little Arthur MacArthur, the four-year-old son of General and Mrs. Douglas MacArthur, is having his first taste of real life. According to a friend of the MacArthurs, who recently returned from the Philippines, the adored son of the "Hero of the Hour" had never been allowed outside of his own back yard. Prior to the war, all callers who visited the MacArthurs at their penthouse on the top of the Manila Hotel, were required to bathe their hands in disinfectant before they were permitted to view the MacArthur "heir." Up until Mrs. MacArthur and her son were compelled to leave Manila when it was invaded by the Japs, little Arthur had never been allowed to leave his home at the hotel and had never set foot on terra firma. Several days ago, little Arthur was reported celebrating his fourth birthday in an air raid shelter at Corregidor.

Frank "Everything is made for Love" Boykin and Mrs. Boykin entertained at a "love feast" in honor of governor and Mrs. Frank Dixon while they were in Washington last week. The table, which was set for sixty, was placed in the sunroom on the top floor of the Washington Hotel. Here you have a panorama of the White House, the Capitol, the Washington Monument, and most of official Washington; it is a beautiful sight.

Between courses, slides of Bellingrath Gardens in Mobile, Alabama, were shown to the guests.

The remainder of the evening was interspersed by "Love Speeches" and Bouquets from the "one and only" Frank Boykin to his guests. "Come up here, Juliet, leave Romeo behind—I want to have my picture taken with you." "Where is that good-looking Hamilton woman? She ought to be in this picture!" "Mrs. Bankhead—oh, Mrs. Bankhead—we must have that lovely wife of Senator Bankhead in this, too!" And so the photographer who had been hired for the occasion flashed many a dozen films as the evening wore on.

MARCH 8, 1942

As I write tonight, Washington is having its first official ten-hour blackout.

A little while ago I went outdoors to check our windows for possible telltale streaks of light. It gave me the queerest feeling to see our City suddenly take on a ghoulish look. The streetlights have been painted black, with only a small ring of light left at the bottom of the globe.

There are sandbags piled at the windows of the first floor of our apartment building and a First Aid Room, fully equipped with hospital bed and medical supplies, awaits its first casualty.

On my closet shelf are flashlights, cans of soup and a Sterno heater. I suppose I am about as well prepared as the next one, but in my heart I am hoping that air raids won't come to us with the spring thaws. If they do come to this country, I feel that we as Americans can live through them just as our forefathers survived the long hard winter of Valley Forge, and our grandparents the tragic days of reconstruction in the Southland.

To me the most fascinating days in American history are those of our pioneers. For those of us who are so fortunate, the opportunity may again be ours to build a new world of peace from a wilderness of destruction.

The annual Cherry Blossom Fete of Washington has been indefinitely postponed due to the war situation. The excuse given was that the Capitol could no longer house the thousands of tourists who come each year to view the blossoms.

In 1912, the Mayor of the city of Tokyo, Japan, sent to Mrs. William Howard Taft, who was then our First Lady, several hundred cherry trees. The trees were presented to Mrs. Taft by Ambassador Chinda as gift to the United Stares and a token of good will and friendship. Mrs. Taft and Vicountess Chinda, wife of the Japanese Ambassador, planted the first cherry trees on the banks of the Potomac around the Tidal Basin. In past years members of the Japanese Embassy dressed in native costumes and joined with Americans in celebrating the friendly relationship between the two countries. Last year a fanatical group of women chained themselves to a number of these cherry trees that were marked to be cut down to make way for the new Jefferson Memorial. How times do change!

A friend of mine who has just returned from New York told me that the FBI had recently picked up a number of Japanese in Harlem who were preaching a very dangerous doctrine—namely that this is a White Man's War. This same doctrine seems to have succeeded far beyond expectations in Singapore, Burma, and all points East. The one exception, where the natives are really fighting, is in the Philippines. Because of their promised independence in 1946 they feel that they have something to fight for. In this vein, I ran across some very effective propaganda last summer that was being preached in the colored churches in Alabama by a white man of unknown nationality from New York. These things all tie up together with Hitler's plan of divide and conquer.

To add a dash of Tabasco to an otherwise flavorless dish: since fame overtook Douglas MacArthur, his ex-wife, Louise Atwell, who apparently now regrets leaving MacArthur, has nevertheless sought to bask in her former husband's reflected glory. Some think that she either wrote or inspired a series of undignified articles that appeared recently in a Washington paper about her former marriage to MacArthur.

Mrs. Atwell arrived at a party last week, wearing a lovely corsage of gardenias. "These are in honor of my anniversary," she told friends. "Did Lionell Atwell send them to you?" the friends inquired. "Oh no! I meant mine and Doug's anniversary," she told the surprised group.

Mrs. Atwell resides in Washington while Lionel Atwell dwells in parts unknown. But I would bet my last dollar that "Doug" would deeply resent the insinuations that he had remembered "to say it with flowers."

MARCH 1942

Vice President Henry Wallace must be related in some way to Eleanor Roosevelt. He is the only person I know who has an equal amount of physical endurance. Every Sunday before church (weather permitting), he plays tennis, then immediately following lunch he is out on the court again for the remainder of the afternoon. Recently, while vacationing at Atlantic City, he played squash all morning with professional players, tennis all afternoon, and ping pong after dinner that night. He then took a five-mile hike down the boardwalk, just to be able to sleep well. He is constantly after members of the Senate to play handball with him or to take a swim before the session opens every morning.

The Vice President arises early enough each day to play a few sets of tennis before breakfast. Two of his casualties who just couldn't take it are Justice Hugo Black (suffering from a game leg) and Senator William Smathers of New Jersey (whose back was strapped). Both were trying to compete with the Vice President at tennis.

A Spanish tutor arrives daily at the Wallace apartment at eight o'clock to give lessons to the family during breakfast. Mrs. Wallace sits and sips sassafras tea and digests a few Spanish words at the same time. (I didn't know that anyone in Washington had ever heard of sassafras tea outside of "Peter Rabbit" and me.) These Spanish lessons proved a great help to the Vice President and Mrs. Wallace during the frequent visits of South American officials this spring and summer. Certainly it is far more satisfactory to be able to speak the same language as a foreign neighbor than to have to rely on an interpreter. With a clearer understanding of the language and customs of a foreign nation comes a closer unity and cooperation between them and us.

The Wallaces are very conscientious. They are almost Puritanical in their desires to perform their duties to the best of their abilities. The Vice President has presided in the Senate more consistently than any previous Vice President. Mrs. Wallace never misses a Senate Ladies Luncheon (which meets every Tuesday to do Red Cross work) if it can possibly be avoided. She made the statement that although she was the only person permitted under the by-laws of the Senate Ladies Luncheon Club to bring guests, she would not accept a privilege denied the other members of that organization.

Speaking of sassafras tea, the Vice President is a teetotaler. The night Henry Wallace was nominated for the Vice Presidency at the Democratic Convention in Chicago last summer, a few of his Iowa friends dropped by to congratulate him on his success. Knowing that Henry Wallace had always been a personal dry, they were greatly shocked to see a cocktail tray with ice, ginger ale, and glasses brought in. The tray was placed before the Vice President, who proceeded to mix drinks for everyone. A glass was passed to one of the guests, who, upon tasting it, inquired, "Henry, what is this drink?" Whereupon the Vice President replied, "Iced tea and ginger ale—don't you think it refreshing?" It was quite a celebration.

At Easter time the Vice President sent each member of the Senate a bag of hybrid seed corn, a product of his many years of research work for the benefit of the farmer. In his spare time Henry Wallace is working on the problem that will confront America when peace is restored in the world. He has a creative mind and is an indefatigable worker.

Both of the Wallaces are shy and have very little small talk—their minds are too full of important things to remember to ask, "How are the children?" And yet once they make friends, they keep them.

Once in a while I see Mrs. Wallace in Rock Creek Park walking a dark gray sheep dog (maybe it is a French poodle—I'm not that familiar with dogs). At any rate it is a large shaggy dog with hair in its eyes. Which reminds me of a good family story. Last winter Mrs. Otis Bland of Virginia stopped our son Lister on the street. "Do you have any little boys or girls near you to play with, Lister?" Whereupon Lister shook his head sadly. "Well, you ought to have a little brother or sister as a playmate. Which would you rather have?" Lister thought a minute and then said, "I'd rather have a dog." He got the dog (a red cocker spaniel).

It seems I missed my guess about the presidency of the Senate. Instead of Kenneth McKellar, Senator Carter Glass was accorded the honor of president pro tempore of the Senate. Senator McKellar wanted to run for that office when Pat Harrison was elected, but since Pat had been defeated for the leadership by Barkley several years ago, McKellar was persuaded not to run against Senator Harrison. McKellar has been in ill health this year and it may be he did not desire the position at this time—or perhaps he thought there might be a jinx on the position with the recent deaths of both Key Pittman and Pat Harrison. Senator Glass is over eighty years old but is a bridegroom of a year. His wife is one of the most charming women in Washington. This winter I saw her at a reception. The dress she was wearing, pale blue chiffon with pink roses appliquéd on the skirt, was the most outstanding at the party. With her soft white hair as a frame for her sweet gentle face and a complexion like porcelain, she was as exquisite as a rare cameo.

According to their friends, Senator Glass has attended more social functions since his marriage than in the twenty years previous. Woodrow Wilson once said of him, "If Carter Glass could talk out of both sides of his mouth, I would pity his enemies." (Senator Glass suffered a partial facial paralysis many years ago.) Yet Mrs. Glass entertains her friends by telling them "how sweet the Senator is." (My compliments to Mrs. Glass.)

An amusing tale came to my ears recently. It seems that shortly before the Glass wedding took place, Senator William Smathers of New Jersey jokingly told the Senior Senator from Virginia that in the event Mrs. Smathers gave birth to a son, the child should be named "Carter Glass Smathers." Realizing upon the birth of his son that he had been taken seriously by the Virginia Senator, Senator Smathers found a "way out." He composed a letter to this effect: "My dear Senator Glass: Congratulations! etc. After reading the announcement of your marriage in today's paper, Mrs. Smathers and I have decided that now that you have taken unto yourself a wife and may have use for the name, we are withdrawing the offer to name our son 'Carter Glass.'" Both Senator Glass and his wife were tickled by the implication.

MARCH 29, 1942

Gen. Jonathan M. Wainwright, who was left in command of the Philippines when General MacArthur made his spectacular escape to Australia, is a well-known personality in Washington.

General Wainwright served from 1936 to 1938 as Commanding Officer of the Cavalry Regiment at Ft. Myer, Virginia. While stationed there, he and his attractive wife, who were great horse lovers, developed a horse show that was equal in perfection to any similar exhibition in the world.

The horse shows were held every Friday evening during the spring months in the Riding Hall of the Post. The audience was drawn from the Diplomatic Corps, members of both Houses of Congress, the President's Cabinet, and high ranking Army and Navy officials and their wives. Almost every one of importance in Washington at one time or another has attended the Ft. Myer horse shows.

The performance itself, which was "set to music," was as brilliant and colorful as the audience that witnessed it. There were the "cake walking" horses; the hunter jumping gaily over hedges and through hoops of fire; the wild west show; and a perfectly trained group of acrobats who tumbled from a horse's back and then mounted again as easily as bareback circus riders—all while the horses continued around the ring at full speed.

To remind one that this was an Army post, there were the more serious military feats: the sham battle in which machine guns were brought in and set up and fired at a miniature village; a mounted battery moving in intricate design with perfect precision at full speed ahead; and lastly a crack troop of Cavalry who entered with many flags flying and halted in front of the Commanding Officer to receive a salute while "The Star Spangled Banner" was played.

Following these exhibitions, a reception was held for the visiting dignitaries and the officers and their wives. General and Mrs. Wainwright always headed the receiving line and saw that the guests were introduced to one another. These affairs were the means of promoting a feeling of friendship between civilians, diplomats, and our service groups.

Because of the excellence of the Ft. Myer horse shows, tickets, which were given away to the first requests, had to be asked for weeks ahead in order to obtain them.

Besides the wide reputation that was gained through the horse show, the Ft. Myer Cavalry Regiment is known as the official "Honor Guard." For generations it has been used in the Inaugural Parade as an escort for the President. It was also used for the funeral of William Howard Taft. Washingtonians have thrilled at the sight of the Ft. Myer Cavalry at each "Army Day Parade," now postponed until after the war, and on many other important occasions which call for a bit of glamour. (Many of the soldiers who rode in the horse shows were shipped out to the Philippines with Gen. Wainwright—they were a part of the Walk to Bataan.)

It is at Ft. Myer that the Chief of Staff of our Army resides. General MacArthur spent five years there, in the red brick mansion that is provided for the head of our General Staff, before he was retired. It is possible that the friendship between MacArthur and Wainwright began at Ft. Myer while they were stationed there.

There is a superstition in the Wainwright family that so long as General Wainwright carries an old silver watch which belonged to his father, Major Robert Powell Page Wainwright, the Japs might just as well save their shells, for no harm can come to him. I am inclined to believe that "Skinny" Wainwright (as he is called) will hold the port until MacArthur makes good his promise, "I will return."

Ft. Myer adjoins our National Cemetery, Arlington. Someone asked me not long ago how General Lee's homeplace happened to be made into a national cemetery. At the outbreak of the War Between the States, General Lee was offered the position of Commander-in-Chief of the Federal Army. Turning this offer down, Lee resigned his commission in the Federal Army and went home, where he became Chief of Staff of Northern Virginia.

It seems that while Lee was a student at West Point he had a friend, General Meigs, who deeply resented the fact that Lee chose to fight on the side of the Confederacy. One day Meigs was engaged in battle near Lee's home at Arlington and suffered severe losses. Enraged by his seeming defeat, he said, "Damn Lee. I will get even with him. I will make a Yankee graveyard out of his home place." Whereupon Meigs ordered all his dead soldiers buried at Arlington. From then on all soldiers killed in that vicinity were interred on the property which was later confiscated from the Lee family and turned into a national cemetery.

SPRING MUST BE JUST around the corner. The willows are budding out and the forsythia, the first flower to bloom here each year, is turning yellow. Spring always makes me homesick for Alabama. Not that Washington isn't beautiful, with its cherry blossoms, flowering magnolias and dogwood. Azaleas grow in profusion here, though not as luxurious as in Mobile.

APRIL 5, 1942

Thurman Arnold, our able and fearless Assistant Attorney General who is very much in the news these days, believes in battling all whom he considers foes of the preservation of American Democracy. Last month he hit labor, industry, and monopolies equally severe blows.

For many years Thurman Arnold has worked tirelessly in his efforts to break up monopolies, in particular those trusts that were part of a world combine. Three years ago, I was present when he explained to a group of friends the pending disaster to America because of these combines or cartels of American firms with Germany.

As a result of the shortsightedness on the part of certain American firms, we today have shortages in synthetic rubber, optical instruments of all kinds (including telescopes and periscopes), certain necessary drugs, and many other essential war materials. All of these articles were manufactured in Germany, some by use of American patents, while American manufacturers agreed not to compete in these fields if Germany would agree to a protected monopoly for certain American firms on other specified products. In this way the market was greatly restricted and the control of prices maintained.

For several years Arnold has had a suit pending against the Aluminum Company of America, which is still pending in the U.S. Supreme Court. This company claims not to have been a member of the cartels; nevertheless one of their affiliates, the Aluminum Company of Canada, was connected with German interests in a world combine.

At the beginning of World War I, the price of aluminum rose from 18.6 cents a pound to 64.6 cents a pound. Since the Reynolds Metals Company in Alabama has been operating as a competitor of the Aluminum Company of America, we have had a drop from 20.6 cents a pound to the present low price of 15.6 cents a pound. When you consider the vast number of planes produced today, these price lists seem incredible.

Thurman Arnold has gone on record as saying that when the war is over, the United States Government should prevent a continuation of the "pooling of patents" and the entrance of American firms into cartels with foreign interests since such world combines hamper progress and production in America.

To give you a "pen picture" of Thurman Arnold—he is a rugged individualist, and a man of honor who has the highest of principles. It matters not whom he offends as long as he feels that he is performing his duty. In stature he is rather heavy set. His complexion is sallow, and there are great circles around his deep dark eyes. The former Yale law professor looks as if he is a bit weary with overwork, but this does not subdue his enthusiasm for his job.

My favorite story on Arnold is: He and I both attended a large tea at the Russian Embassy and as he left the party and started down the front steps I overheard the doorman (the one seen at all Embassy parties) ask Judge Arnold, "Shall I call your car, sir?"

"Yes, go ahead and call it if you like." Then mischievous Judge Arnold added, "But it won't come."

It is a difficult task to transfer to paper the vivid personalities of the Arnold family; however, I will start with a splash of red—red dots, that is. (The following appeared in the column of Hope Riding Miller in the *Washington Post*.)

On the evening of the day of Pearl Harbor, young Thurman, Jr., was at home with his ears glued to the radio when an announcement came over the air ordering all service men to appear in uniform the next day. Thurman, Jr., who had enlisted in the Navy a short time before and was at home for a visit, found to his chagrin that he was minus a black tie. He searched the house, going through his own and his father's effects, with sad results. It was then ten o'clock on a Sunday night. What should he do? The Assistant Attorney General, being a resourceful man, had an inspiration. He produced a black tie with red dots on it. The two of them—father and son—sat up half the night blacking out the red dots with ink.

There is no more delightful conversationalist in Washington than Mrs. Thurman Arnold. She sparks! As a guest or as a hostess, Francis is charming.

Most of the Arnold parties are informal and impromptu. "Someone sent us a turkey this morning—can you come to dinner tonight?" or "This is Frances Arnold—there is a touch of spring in the air today, and the daffodils look particularly lovely—can't you drive out and sit in the garden this afternoon?" The invited guests always accept if it is possible on such short notice, for they expect a good time and are never disappointed.

The Arnolds live in an old farmhouse that is known as the Dower

House at McLean, Virginia. It is rambling and quaint, but I daresay the family shivers in winter from an inadequate heating system. Furnished throughout with rare antiques, the home still has a comfortable and livable look.

There are the ruins of an old chimney in the front yard, a milk cow named "Angel" wandering about the garden chewing grass, a hedge of lilacs, and a profusion of wisteria climbing over the treetops.

In the garage there are three ancient Packard cars. The Assistant Attorney General showed them to me and explained with great pride, "I only paid $25.00 apiece for them at the second-hand dealers. One is for Frances, one for the servants, and one for me."

With the tire situation what it is today, the Arnolds are planning to move this summer, and have taken a house in the city of Alexandria. Wherever it is, I am sure it will have an atmosphere all its own—but poor Angel, I am wondering if she will take to life in the city, or if she will be forced to sacrifice "her all" for the war effort.

APRIL 12, 1942

Washingtonians will be at a loss this year to determine just when spring has officially arrived—no cherry blossom fete, no White House Easter egg rolling, no Daughters of the American Revolution.

For fifty-five consecutive years the DARs have held their annual Continental Congress in their national shrine "Constitution Hall" in the city of Washington. Every Easter Monday, a horde of five thousand Daughters descend on the Nation's Capital and capture all available hotel accommodations, all elevators, all taxicabs, and a large portion of the restaurants for the week following.

Due to the present crowded conditions in Washington, the Daughters, who are always eager to cooperate in any national emergency, announced through their President General, Mrs. William H. Pouch, that they had decided to take the convention to Chicago this year.

The florists in Washington no doubt will wear bands of mourning for the departed Daughters for it was no uncommon sight to see three or four corsages on the same bosom amidst a collection of ancestor bars, DAR pins, and official ribbons.

One of the most worthwhile projects sponsored by the Daughters is the Kate Duncan Smith School for mountain boys and girls in North Alabama. This school was started by Kate Duncan Smith, the mother of Mrs. Sam Earle of Birmingham.

Washington doesn't have a climate; it has weather. An eighteen-inch snow (the second snowfall of the year) covered the Capital City on Palm Sunday. Two days later the snow had melted and the cherry trees were in bloom around the Tidal Basin. By Easter Sunday, Washingtonians were sweltering under 83 degrees of sunshine and discarding all wraps for the Easter parade.

Mrs. Roosevelt was too busy to purchase a new Easter outfit, but many other persons appeared in colorful attire. The gayest costume I saw was worn by the wife of Senator Carter Glass of Virginia. Mrs. Glass was seen leaving the Mayflower Hotel looking particularly "Easterly," wearing a purple ensemble with purple hat, shoes and corsage. Both the hat and the shoulder corsage were of Parma violets.

The second prize of the Easter season goes to General Edwin Watson, secretary and personal friend of the President. With his brown tweed suit, which was flecked with yellow, General Watson wore a necktie of red, yellow, green, and blue ovals, which looked for all the world like a nest of Easter Eggs. By way of apology, he exclaimed, "Someone sent a batch of ties to the White House; two for the Boss, two for Steve Early, and two for me. I got there in time for the leavings."

The Society of Sponsors of the United States Navy held their annual meeting at the Mayflower Hotel on April 7th and 8th. This organization is composed of those women who have christened ships of the United States Navy that are large enough to carry guns. The purpose of the Society is to care for as many as possible of the widows and orphans of the "men who go down to sea."

The President, Mrs. Russell Langdon (Adrian Semple, formerly of Alabama), presided over the annual luncheon of new members. Among the new members of the organization are myself, and Mrs. Cooper Green,

William L. and Etta Copeland McCormick, parents
of Henrietta Fontaine McCormick.

The McCormick family home in Eufaula, Alabama.

Above: Henrietta F. McCormick's grandparents, Dr. William P. and Mary Flewellen Copeland. *Below:* Etta Copeland McCormick with daughters Mary and Henrietta (right).

Congressman Lister Hill and Henrietta McCormick Hill
surrounded by the U.S. Army Band on their wedding day,
February 20, 1928, in Columbus, Georgia.

Congressman Lister Hill and Henrietta McCormick Hill
on the boardwalk in Atlantic City, 1928.

Above: The Hill family in 1937. From left, Congressman J. Lister Hill, L. Lister Hill, Henrietta McCormick Hill, and Henrietta Fontaine Hill. *Below:* The family on an NBC radio program in 1945. From left, Henrietta McCormick Hill, Henrietta Fontaine Hill, the interviewer, young Lister, and the Senator.

Above: Henrietta McCormick Hill with Henrietta Fontaine Hill and L. Lister Hill at the beach.

Left: Henrietta McCormick Hill.

Above: The Hill family at dinner, 1960s. From left, Catharine Hill, L. Lister Hill, Henrietta McCormick Hill, and Senator Lister Hill.

Below: Henrietta McCormick Hill christening the *U.S.S. Alabama*, February 16, 1942.

Henrietta McCormick Hill (right) listening to her husband,
Senator Lister Hill, give a speech in 1957.

Above: Senator Lister Hill and Henrietta McCormick Hill, 1950s.
Below: On a Mediterranean cruise, 1951.

Above: The Hills with fellow Alabamian, U.S. Supreme Court Justice Hugo Black. *Below:* With Vice President Alben Barkley. From left, Mrs. Barkley, Senator Lister Hill, Vice President Barkley, and Henrietta McCormick Hill.

Above:
Senator
Lister Hill
at the 1952
Democratic
National
Convention.

Right:
Senator Hill
greeting
a farmer
in south
Alabama,
1962.

President Kennedy signs into law Senator Hill's bill establishing the National Library of Medicine at the National Institutes of Health. In 1968, a joint resolution of Congress designated a part of the National Library as the Lister Hill National Center for Biomedical Communications.

Grandsons—
Right: Lister
Hubbard,
fishing, 1966.
Center: Henrietta
McCormick
Hill with Clark
Hubbard. *Bottom:*
Senator Hill with
Clark (left) and
Lister Hubbard.

wife of Birmingham's Mayor, who recently christened the Cruiser, *The City of Birmingham*. Lister delivered the principal address at the luncheon.

On Army Day, April 6th, the Nation's Capital was inundated by the MacArthur popularity wave, which has swept the country.

Contrary to the usual custom, there was no Army Day parade in Washington this year, but a gala event at which laurel wreaths were placed upon the brow of the hero of the hour, General Douglas MacArthur, which was unveiled at a large gathering of distinguished persons at the Mayflower Hotel on Monday afternoon.

Mrs. Arthur MacArthur, the General's sister-in-law, was assisted by Mrs. Paul McNutt (wife of the former Commissioner of the Philippines) in pulling the cord that brought to view the bronze likeness of the famous general. There was much applause, and many "*ohs* and *ahs;*" and everyone congratulated the young sculptor, Nison Tregor. There was a brief speech by William Howard Hoeffer, who had commissioned Tregor to do the bust for the Military Academy at West Point, and a fitting acceptance by Major General William Connor speaking on behalf of the U.S. Military Academy.

The Army Day Message was delivered by General Albert Lyman Cox, and the message from the Philippines by the Resident Commissioner, J.M. Elizalde, who said, "You call him the hero of the world. We still call him MacArthur of Bataan."

Next, Dr. Herbert Vere Evatt, the Australian representative, arose and spoke with equal eloquence: "MacArthur has a monument more lasting than bronze. He is the savior of all free people in the Pacific."

Three hundred invitations were issued but as usual at a Washington party, there were four hundred gatecrashers. (It takes a brave person to give a tea in Washington and put it in the paper beforehand.)

Dan Cupid was full of smiles last Saturday when three prominent Alabamians were joined together in wedlock; Miss Margaret Ellis, the daughter of Mr. and Mrs. Handy Ellis of Columbiana, to Ensign John Copeland of Anniston; and Miss Elizabeth Bailey, the daughter of Senator and Mrs. Josiah Bailey of North Carolina, to William Primm, Jr. of Montgomery.

The Ellis-Copeland wedding took place in the City of Washington at the New York Presbyterian Church in the historic Lincoln Chapel, while the Bailey-Primm nuptials were performed in Raleigh, North Carolina.

The Lincoln Chapel (where Lincoln attended church) is furnished in the Victorian era and made a perfect setting for the dainty Margaret Ellis, who was a vision of loveliness in a tulle veil with a lace coronet, and a white lace wedding gown, which was fashioned over a hoop skirt.

The guests were few and the wedding was a simple affair but as the bride said, "Since I plan to be a bride only once, I was determined to have a wedding dress even if there were only two persons present for the ceremony."

Due to the war, Ensign Copeland, who is stationed somewhere in the New England states, could not reach Alabama for the wedding and then have time left over for a honeymoon, all of which was sad news to the bride's father. Because of his political race for Lieutenant Governor, Handy Ellis had to forego the pleasure of seeing his daughter married. Many are the penalties of war and of politics!

By way of the grapevine, I hear that intimate friends of Senator Tom Connelly of Texas and of Mrs. Sheppard (widow of Senator Morris Sheppard) seems to think there is no doubt that a wedding is brewing. Recently Mrs. Sheppard visited her daughter in Philadelphia. Upon her return to Washington the Texas Senator boarded the train at Silver Spring, Maryland, just for the ride!

THE DEDICATION OF THE recently completed Jefferson Memorial, which was to have taken place on April 13, the birth date of Thomas Jefferson, has been postponed until next year because of the war.

The Jefferson Memorial was designed by John Russell Pope, but bears a remarkable resemblance to "the old rotunda" which is used as a library at the University of Virginia, and to Monticello, Jefferson's home in Charlottesville; both buildings were designed by Jefferson himself. The new memorial is round, circled by Corinthian columns, and topped by a vast dome.

The shrine was built to commemorate the 200th anniversary of Jefferson's birth date, sits on the banks of the Tidal Basin, and communes with the memorials of the illustrious Presidents George Washington and Abraham Lincoln. Ironically they stand surrounded by the famed Japanese cherry trees—unblushingly, unashamed in their beauty this year.

At some future date when the sculptor, Rudolph Evans, has put the finishing touches to his work, a giant statue of Jefferson will stand in majesty and dignity as the only adornment to the interior of the shrine. Engraved within the dome are Jefferson's immortal words written to a friend in 1800: "I have sworn on the altar of God eternal hostility against every form of tyranny over the mind of man."

Although Jefferson had many responsibilities and honors bestowed upon him during his lifetime—having served as a member of the House of Burgesses of Virginia, as Governor of the State of Virginia, Minister to France, Secretary of State under Washington, Vice President under John Adams, and finally as third President of the United States—the only inscription he wished upon this tombstone were the things which he had done for his fellow man, for these were the things of which he was the proudest, "Author of the Declaration of Independence, Author of the Virginia Statute of Religious Freedom, and Father of the University of Virginia."

Jefferson believed that the way to preserve the ideals for which he fought, "Freedom of Speech, Freedom of the Press, and Freedom to Worship God in one's chosen way," was to educate the masses on whom the hope of continued freedom depends. Because Jefferson practiced what he preached ("Never to engage while in public office in any kind of enterprise for the improvement of my fortune"), he died a poor man.

Shortly before his death he was forced to sell his private library (some 13,000 volumes) to Congress for the sum of $24,000—just half of its original value. This was the nucleus of the Congressional Library of today.

Some years ago the Curator of the Library showed me this priceless collection. On the margins of many of the volumes are notations in Jefferson's own hands. It is interesting to know this amazing fact—many of the volumes were in Greek, Latin, French, and Italian, the notations in each case matching the language of the book in which they were written.

During this week of the 200th Anniversary of the birth of Jefferson, it would be well for all of us to pause and reflect upon the life and sayings of the founder of America's democracy; for it was he who gave us the principles of Government for which every American should be proud to fight to preserve.

APRIL 19, 1942

Shortly after Pearl Harbor, the German, Italian, Bulgarian, and Japanese Diplomats in this country were all transported to the resort hotels in Virginia and West Virginia, to await deportation to their homelands.

The two resorts which are being used for these unwelcomed guests are "The Greenbrier Hotel" in White Sulphur Springs, West Virginia, and "The Homestead Hotel" at Hot Springs, Virginia. For years the aristocracy of the South made annual tours of the Virginia springs to take the cure at "The Hot," "The Sweet," "The Warm," and "The White." These planters brought with them their daughters and sons, for this was one of America's richest marriage markets.

Many years ago, Lister and I spent a few days at "The White" and "The Hot" as the guests of his parents. The minimum rate at that time was $18.00 a day. "The White" is tucked in between the Blue Ridge Mountains, and has been a famous resort since 1830. "The Hot," located forty miles away and just across the mountain from "The White," is equally as luxurious a hotel. The Japanese Diplomats are interned at "The Hot." It is rumored that the waiters at "The Hot" are almost in a state of revolt; the reason—the Japs give no tips.

Word comes from White Sulphur Springs that the interned German, Italian, and Bulgarian Diplomats who are quartered there are daily storing away pounds of flesh. Could it be that these diplomats are eating all they can, while they can, against the dreadful day when they bid goodbye to the land of "life, liberty, and the pursuit of happiness?"

Rumblings of dissatisfaction at America's finest hostelry have reached the Capital. The Germans have let out a howl since the Japs are being transferred from "The Hot" to "The White." The Italians and Bulgarians will be moved to Asheville, North Carolina, thus leaving the Germans with their Axis partners, the Japs. It will be like tying two cats together to watch the fur fly.

My special spy tells me that neither the Germans nor the Japs are in a hurry to set sail for their native lands. They are too well situated here as the guests of Uncle Sam. I have been told that the date of the departure for the Germans is not too far distant—sometime between the 20th and 25th of April.

An officer of the Swiss army sent to the United States to negotiate for Germany in the exchange of German and American diplomats arrived in Washington the middle of March. This Swiss officer, who expected to make the return trip immediately, has been held up by innumerable delays and infinite details. One of the delays was caused by the decision of several South American countries to send all of their ejected German diplomats to the U.S. to sail on the same ship as those who were harbored here.

The American diplomats who have been interned in Germany are scheduled to sail from Portugal at the same time that the Germans bid goodbye to the Statue of Liberty. When the boatload of diplomats set sail from the United States, the only protection against friend or foe will be one word—*Diplomats*—printed in large letters in conspicuous places on the ship.

APRIL 1942

For months citizens of Washington have seen soldiers on leave in the Nation's Capital sleeping on the benches of Union Station, the public parks, and in movie lounges. A perturbed group of patriotic women who were shocked by their seeming neglect decided to band together to alleviate, if possible, a distressing situation.

After eight weeks of concentrated effort, the ladies are happy to announce that the President's reception room at Union Station is being converted into a lounge for transient service men. The formal dedication ceremonies will be held on May 10th.

An organization known as the Washington Civilian Recreational Service Committee is responsible for the movement to provide adequate accommodations for the service men. Serving on the committee as Honorary Chairmen are Mrs. Franklin D. Roosevelt, Mrs. Henry Wallace, and Mrs. Woodrow Wilson, and as Acting Chairman, Mrs. Lionel Atwell. Affiliated with this group are the Senate Ladies, Congressional Club, many Army and Navy wives, and various civilian groups.

Because extreme caution is necessary in safeguarding troop movements, each person who volunteered for service at the Union Station Lounge was required to register at the USO as an extra precaution. The lists of applicants were then carefully checked by the FBI.

The President's reception room has long been used by the State Department as a place of "official welcoming" for visiting royalty, Ambassadors arriving at their posts of duty, and to foreign missions sent to the United States from the four corners of the earth. It was here that the President and Mrs. Roosevelt greeted King George and Queen Elizabeth just three years ago.

The new lounge is 500 by 50 feet in dimension and has been redecorated by Elise Cobb Wilson. An attractive feature of the decorations is the huge maps papered on the sidewalls. These maps are large enough in size for any soldier boy to locate his own little crossroad town.

Provided at the reception rooms are easy chairs, radios, writing desks with free stationery and greeting cards, lockers, and washrooms. On the floor above, five hundred beds and a small hospital unit have been made available to any serviceman who might desire to use them. Directly outside the lounge a canteen will be in operation on a 24-hour-a-day schedule.

For entertainment, sightseeing buses, free theatre tickets, and an occasional invitation to dinner now await Uncle Sam's boys who have long been neglected in their National Capital.

Since Admiral Leahy, our Ambassador to Vichy, France, has been called home for consultation (many think permanently), young Douglas MacArthur, nephew and namesake of General MacArthur, is among those persons left in charge of the American Embassy. MacArthur has served as military attaché at the Embassy for the past five years. He is accompanied by his wife and five year old daughter. His wife is the former Laura Barkley, daughter of the majority leader of the Senate, Alben Barkley of Kentucky.

As long as it is possible to do so, Mrs. Barkley sent canned milk and foods to her daughter. Now the only contact the MacArthurs have with their families is entirely by cable or through the Embassy.

The Barkleys are very proud of the fact that their son, David, who has served with the Army Air Corps for the past year and a half, has just received his Captaincy.

A disheartening story sent from Australia tells of the rampant disease in Bataan Island during the capitulation of that valiant little fighting force. According to reports, ten thousand persons with malaria or dysentery were confined to the two field hospitals. In many instances, both diseases struck the patients. An additional ten thousand milder cases were laid up in the Army camps. The rainy season had set in, making mosquitoes more prevalent and—food having been reduced to a scant, unbalanced diet—the two diseases played great havoc in both the American and Filipino ranks.

As the story goes, it was the absence of quinine and other drugs (and not the lack of ammunition) that forced the surrender of the tired men on Bataan Island.

Several days ago I met Mrs. Francis Cox, who, as the wife of the Episcopal missionary Reverend Cox, had spent eighteen years in Shanghai. Reverend Cox was associated with Bishop Tucker and was the head of the St. John University in Shanghai. Mrs. Cox was ordered evacuated from China last spring, along with other American women. Her husband remained behind to carry on his work with the Chinese.

At the time I saw Mrs. Cox, it had been four months since she had any communication from her husband. Her letters to him had been returned. Occasionally some small bit of information concerning him reaches her through the Red Cross.

In view of what happened at Bataan, I thought this story Mrs. Cox told me was extremely interesting: "The Japs are allowing Americans caught in China to live in their own homes. These Americans are still prisoners of war, but the Japs have washed their hands of the responsibility of feeding their prisoners. Each person must shift for himself. No drugs are given to these prisoners. People in America do not realize what it means to be without medicines. When summer comes, I fear for my husband's health. For years he has suffered with malaria and with no quinine available, the situation looks very tragic. There are many persons who will die this year of dysentery, malaria, cholera, and typhoid fever."

This brave woman said that she was only living to get back to China. It seems that the Japs prefer to let these people die the slow way.

The Senate of the United States can boast of two missionaries in its ranks. Senator and Mrs. Elbert Thomas of Utah spent the first fifteen years of their married life as missionaries in Japan.

I spent all day Wednesday in the soldiers lounge at Union Station checking baggage for the servicemen who wished to leave their belongings with us for a few hours between trains. Oh, how my feet and back ached.

MAY 1942

Mrs. John Bankhead, wife of the Senator, deserted us in April. Every year when spring comes she begins to dream of the daffodils and iris in her yard and to smell the honeysuckle. From then on the Senator might just as well bid her goodbye. I imagine her grandchildren have something to do with her homesickness.

Mrs. Will Bankhead, our beloved Speaker's wife, came back to Washington to accept a position as curator of public monuments—the Lincoln Memorial, Washington Monument, and Jefferson Memorial (not yet completed). After two months she gave it up and returned to Jasper. I believe she couldn't bear the memories she had in Washington.

I sometimes feel sorry for the official wives in Washington. Of course their husbands stay so busy they don't have time for such trite things as homesickness.

When the National Democratic Women's Club held their annual spring festival this year, Miss Julia Ann Sparkman, the lovely young daughter of Congressman and Mrs. Sparkman, was chosen to represent

"Miss America." Julia Ann wore a white tulle dress with yards and yards of material in the skirt—she was a picture of loveliness. The theme of the festival was "Pan America." Each South American country was represented by a native of that country, in most cases by a daughter of a diplomat. These girls all wore colorful, beautiful native costumes. The Panamanian representative won the prize that was awarded by Mrs. Roosevelt.

Congressman Luther Patrick pulled a fast one the other day by picketing the "Peace Pickets" at the White House and peeling potatoes at the same time. Speaking of the "Peace Pickets," they have kept up their march night and day for over a month. The other day my taxi driver (the source of all information for most Washingtonians) told me that the "Peace Pickets" all had foreign names and wouldn't fight to defend America, even if invaded.

MAY 1942

Eleanor Roosevelt unintentionally threw the 75th Club (a Congressional organization) into a state of panic last Thursday when she arrived forty minutes earlier than expected at the Club's annual luncheon for which she was the honor guest. Mrs. Roosevelt appeared unattended in the lobby of the Kennedy-Warren where the party was held, and stood around unobserved for fifteen minutes.

A reception committee had been appointed to greet the First Lady and to escort her to the place of honor in the dining hall, whereupon the Marine Band was to strike up "The Star Spangled Banner." Because of Mrs. Roosevelt's early arrival, the President of the Club, Mrs. Laurence Arnold, wife of Congressman Arnold of Illinois, was all in a dither. Eventually the situation cleared and Mrs. Roosevelt arose to give one of the finest talks I have ever heard her make.

The proceeds from the luncheon this year were donated to the "Save the Children Club." The Washington branch of this federation is sponsoring a day nursery for children of defense workers who cannot afford a full-time nurse at home. Mrs. Roosevelt is a former president of the Club and is particularly interested now in the movement to start day nurseries throughout the country in industrial areas.

This looks like an excellent opportunity for many patriotic American women who are anxious to help in the national emergency. To quote Mrs. Roosevelt: "Juvenile crime is on the increase. What we do for the youth today will be a great factor in winning the war."

As Mrs. Roosevelt left the luncheon, the reception committee that failed "to greet" did their dead-level best to keep up with our First Lady to bid her "adieu"—the last I saw of the committee they were panting, three yards behind her.

Mrs. Henry Wallace stayed behind for a few minutes' chat with Madam Chautemps, wife of the former French Premier. She departed very much embarrassed because the horn on her car, a new buff-colored convertible sedan, had stuck.

FIVE FRENCH CAREER DIPLOMATS resigned last week from the Vichy Embassy Staff in Washington in protest of the return to power of Pierre Laval. These Frenchmen have now cast their lots with General de Gaulle, leader of the Free French Movement that wishes to continue the war against Hitler.

Colonel Emanuel E. Lombard, former Military Attaché of the French Embassy in Washington, likewise cabled General de Gaulle in London, "asking the honor of serving with your command. Petain's recall of Pierre Laval shattered my illusions about the former French leader. It is my duty now to go with those who represent France and the French spirit," Lombard is quoted as saying.

Colonel Lombard, who was attached to the French Embassy here for fifteen years, resigned his commission shortly after the fall of France when the Nazi-controlled Henri Haye was sent to replace former Ambassador Saint Quentin: "There are very few differences between the policies of the Vichy regime and Nazi Germany."

One of the few French officers to have been awarded the American Distinguished Service Cross, Colonel Lombard also holds the Croix de Guerre and is an officer in the Legion of Honor. Last spring Colonel Lombard applied for American citizenship; it has always been evident that he was unhappy over the fate of his native land.

JUNE 1942

Visiting in Washington this past week was a most unusual character, a Mrs. Elmhurst of Devonshire, England. She had recently accompanied her husband on a lecture tour of the United States in the interest of British-American agricultural production.

The Elmhursts own and operate a modern farm at Devonshire, and have spent years of experimental work on increased production per acre on their land. Mrs. Elmhurst is an American by birth, being the daughter of one of New York's four hundred, Payne Whitney. She was also one of the charter members of the Junior League of America. At a luncheon several days ago, at which she was the honor guest, Mrs. Elmhurst spoke informally of her experiences during the blitz of London and of conditions in England today.

At present there are three hundred school children who are evacuees of London, billeted on the Elmhurst estate. According to Mrs. Elmhurst, "Even in your own home, no one is allowed more than one bedroom for their private use if additional space in your house is needed to shelter evacuees or persons without homes. There are rows of cots in both my dining room and drawing room, and the kitchen is now a community affair.

"When the night comes the families who live in the country draw into themselves. There is not a ray of light visible, so it would be very dangerous to go prowling about. With no available transportation, visiting one's scattered neighbors in the rural communities is practically prohibited. The rural families have led a very lonely life since the war began.

"In the cities, however, life is just the opposite. The population seems to dread being alone. Society in London is very gay. As many as can obtain space have moved into the hotels and apartment houses. These larger constructions are more resistant to bombings than the individual homes.

"All over England one finds community kitchens where thousands are fed daily. If there is meat available it is sent to these kitchens for the benefit of the many instead of being sold to individuals. Food at these places is comparatively cheap; the service is cafeteria. Because of the long waiting lines no one is allowed to remain in these eating-places longer than ten minutes.

"The first night I went into a bomb shelter, I felt that I could not endure it. The air was foul—there were no sanitary connections—but I soon got used to it, for it seems that the lower the physical being sinks, the higher the spiritual rises. The morale was wonderful. Since that time the air raid shelters have all had sanitary connections put in and are equipped with first aid stations.

"So long as everyone knows that everyone else is doing without, no one minds making the necessary sacrifices to win this war."

The Office of Civilian Defense is making a house-to-house canvass in Washington to find unoccupied rooms for the homeless in case of bombings.

The American Women Volunteers have recently inaugurated a new branch into their organization known as the "Farmerettes." A member of the Board told me that they hoped to get women volunteers to spend their vacations or whatever time they can give on the farms to aid farmers in crop productions this year.

America must feed not only herself but also her allies if this war is to won.

June 1942

Last night I attended the commencement exercise of the National University Law School. This school has been in existence for some forty or more years. Most of the students attend night classes and hold down jobs during the day. There were seven or eight Alabamians to receive law degrees, including one young woman. Out of a class of two hundred and fifty, I would judge seventy were women.

Lister delivered the commencement address. In fifteen minutes' time he told those graduating all they needed to know to become good citizens. It was really a very inspiring speech. I am glad to see that speeches are becoming streamlined. I shall never forget my own commencement—after two hours the orator was just getting warmed up. The University conferred an honorary LL.D. degree upon Lister and I gave him a reception afterwards.

Representative Sam Hobbs and his family went home to Selma for their son Truman's wedding on June 8th. The Alabama delegation gave the bride and groom a handsome silver tray to match the silver service that the Hobbs gave them for a wedding present. Mrs. Hobbs told her friends here that Sam Earle had been courting this young lady since high school days. Somehow the young lady couldn't quite make up her mind, so Mrs. Hobbs decided to play cupid. She took the young lady to visit her son, Sam, in Cleveland, Ohio, where he is working on a case for the FBI How's that for a perfect mother-in-law?

Since writing this letter I find that the Hobbs family met with an automobile accident while returning from the wedding in Selma to Washington on Friday the 13th. Congressman Hobbs and their younger son, Truman, escaped with minor injuries. Mrs. Hobbs had bones in both feet broken and severe lacerations and bruises. Her daughter, Rose, suffered lacerations on her face and bruises. It is thought that the Hobbs will return to Washington in a few days and that Mrs. Hobbs will be taken to Johns Hopkins.

There are five native-born Alabamians in the United States Senate today—Kenneth McKellar of Tennessee, Josh Lee of Oklahoma, Claude Pepper of Florida, and Alabama's own representatives, John Bankhead and Lister Hill. One of these, unless I miss my guess, is most likely to be elected to fill Pat Harrison's former position as president pro tempore of the Senate. Lister, who has continued to preside over the Senate during Pat Harrison's long illness, is already Democratic Whip. With Barkley as majority leader of the Senate, McKellar as president pro tempore, and Lister as whip, the South will still hold her own in the Nation's Capital.

Right now, Senator Josh Lee has quite a problem on his hands. He is engaged in a campaign for re-election against a candidate whose legal name is John Lee. There is a Will Rogers in Congress, who is no doubt a fine Representative of the State of Oklahoma, but his election was purely a tribute to the beloved name of "Will Rogers."

The Russian Ambassador's wife, Madam Litvinoff, has issued invitations for a large "At Home" on next Thursday.

It has been interesting to note the ever-fluctuating popularity in Washington of the various Russian diplomats. For nearly twenty years after the last World War, the magnificent Embassy on Sixteenth Street was boarded up. When the United States finally decided to recognize the U.S.S.R. in 1934 and the Russian Ambassador Trozanovsky arrived in town, all Washington was curious to see this strange creature. The Embassy was redecorated and furnished with the belongings of Catherine the Great. People from all walks of life left cards by the thousands, and were promptly invited to the Embassy to tea. The Trozanovskies soon became one of Washington's most popular host and hostess. Great crowds of people gathered, whenever invited, to sip vodka, eat caviar and sturgeon and the many other delectable delicacies spread before them.

With the invasion of Finland, the Russian Embassy's popularity dwindled overnight and the new Ambassador Oumansky and his wife were snubbed on all occasions.

Little Finland, the only foreign country up to that time to pay back her entire World War I indebtedness to the United States, was for many years very popular with Americans. A man of great personal charm, Hjalmar Procop, represented her at the time. When Finland was invaded by Russia, Washingtonians went overboard trying to raise money for "Finnish Relief." But overnight the picture changed and America found herself allied with Russia against Nazi Germany (the ally of Finland.)

It was not until Germany attacked Russia and Oumansky was recalled that anyone of any importance would have considered accepting Russian hospitality. Now, come Thursday—I dare say—almost everyone who received an invitation for Madam Litvinoff's affair will be on hand and will once more tread the winding stairway that leads straight to the outstretched hands of the representatives of the U.S.S.R. And that is Washington diplomacy! Your friends today are your enemies tomorrow.

Not long ago I heard Senator Alben Barkley tell of his experiences in Russia in 1937. He was a member of a Senatorial group that attended the Inter-Parliamentary Union held that year in Russia. At the completion of the Conference (a Union to discuss International affairs) Senator Barkley and his party hired an old Ford car and motored through Russia.

His talk was the most enlightening one I have heard on the U.S.S.R. The point that impressed me most was this: On Sunday nights Senator Barkley visited numerous churches and heard the most magnificent singing. Not understanding Russian, he did not know what was said, but he understood that a devout religious service was conducted in every church he visited. If there is a seed of religious faith in Russia that can be kept alive, there is hope for her yet.

DECEMBER 7, 1942

Dear Mama,

The lovely box of roses and the bountiful box of gifts arrived in plenty of time for my birthday. If anybody has been spoiled, it is your youngest child; you have always been so sweet and generous with me. I am much more sentimental about my birthday than I am about Christmas. Christmas is the Christ Child's birthday, but December six is my day!

We entertained twenty-two people at a buffet supper last night in honor of the occasion. Your roses made a lovely centerpiece for the dining room table. Among our guests were Mr. and Mrs. Josh Lee of Oklahoma, Senator and Mrs. Worth Clark of Idaho, former Ambassador to Canada James Cromwell, and Justice and Mrs. Hugo Black.

Several of my friends brought me gifts. It was one of the nicest parties I ever had, but may be the last for the duration. I understand that meat and lard are the next items to be rationed. Whipping cream is not to be had in Washington.

The two most attractive guests here last night were the Cowles brothers of Iowa, John and Mike. The family owns the *Des Moines Register*, the *Minneapolis Star*, and *Look Magazine*. Mike has just returned from a plane trip around the world with Wendell Willkie. I have heard that the Cowles financed the trip. It must have been a fascinating experience. Mike seems to think that Russia will defeat the Germans.

Washington is so overrun; you never saw anything like the crowds on the streets. It makes me dizzy to see them milling around. Christmas shopping has been rather hectic; you can't get anywhere near a counter. I don't mind the endless standing in line and doing without things nearly as much as I do the rudeness of people. Some of the clerks are insuffer-able. After all, everybody is living under stress, and the least you can do is try to not make it worse by being disagreeable.

I am quite sure that our butcher takes bribes. I saw a woman give the butcher a five-dollar bill and say, "I will have the same for you next week." She went away with several large sacks of meat. When it came my turn, the butcher swore up and down that all he had was hot dogs. My family and I will eat hot dogs the rest of the war before I offer anyone a bribe.

Look out for four packages of Christmas presents, which I mailed to you. Don't open until Christmas.

Love, H.

Tuesday, January 27, 1943

Walter Bragg Smith is coming to supper tonight and bringing some man with him. Every time Walter drives up from Montgomery, he brings us something good to eat. The last time he came he brought a fruit cake and some grapefruit. Anything to eat is greatly appreciated nowadays. With rationing, and so many people coming to Washington, it is a little hard sometimes to purchase the things you need. We have had several crates of fruit and some ham and country bacon sent us.

Yesterday I was co-hostess to forty-five paratroopers at the Senate res-taurant for luncheon. This group of boys wrote a letter to the *Washington Post* begging somebody to arrange a holiday—perhaps their last—for them before going overseas. All sorts of people gave parties for them. Four senate wives banded together and gave the party at the Capitol. These boys were all trained at Russell County, Alabama. They came to Washington from North Carolina where they had been sent.

There was one boy named Chapman who had a cast on a broken leg that he acquired during a jump. He went around getting different Senators' signatures on his cast and said that he was going to shellac it and send it to his mother after it was removed. It really hurt my heart to see that lovely bunch of kids going away into battle. (This was indeed he last holiday for these paratroopers. I was told they were mistaken for the enemy and shot down by our Navy as they bailed out over Sicily.)

We went to Emily Ligon Foley's for Sunday dinner. It is getting increasingly hard to entertain at all with no ice cream, no butter, no whipping cream. When I think about how the English are being bombed, I think we are very fortunate. Everybody here goes to parties via the bus, or walks, or stays home. For this reason, long dresses are almost out of style.

Mama sent a check. I think I will buy something foolish for a change.

FEBRUARY 18, 1943

Dearest Mama,

Here are the gas tickets I promised you for you birthday. The coupons are for five gallons each. My car has been in the shop and the weather has been so bad that I prefer riding on the bus. We live seven blocks from the bus line. I don't mind the walk when it isn't snowing, but I am afraid I might fall on the ice. So if your birthday present is late this year, please understand. Let the gas coupons be your birthday gift until I can do better.

Dr. Tribble came out to the house a while ago to lance Little Lister's abscessed ear. When the doctor walked in, I had the ironing board set up in his room and was struggling to iron a shirt for Lister. The laundry is sometimes three weeks late. I thought Dr. Tribble would die laughing at me. He said, "I bet you never expected to do washing and ironing when you married a Senator."

He ought to see me scrubbing the floors and cooking sometimes. I have become a pretty good cook. Mrs. Hill wrote that she thought she had a maid who was willing to come to Washington to work for us. The last two she sent stayed only a short time before someone hired them right out of my kitchen.

I hope you will have many happy returns of your birthday. I send you my heart's devotion, but even that is not a gift as you have always had that anyway. You have been the sweetest Mother in the world to me. I don't know how I would have gotten along without you.

Love, H.

Sunday, [Month Unknown] 1943

Dearest Mama,

I am sorry I took so long to write. For four days I had to attend a meeting of the Society of Sponsors of the Navy. As soon as the Sponsors left town I had to work on an Embassy tour for the home for Incurables. Did I tell you I took Mrs. Woodrow Wilson's place on the Board of the Home? There is such a shortage of help at the Home that they have assigned me to work directly with the patients.

Dr. Leslie Glenn, Chaplain of the *Alabama*, wrote me that my ship now has the finest library of any ship in the Navy. We put on a drive for books and money to purchase new books last spring.

September 1943

Young Lister started school this week at the Horace Mann School. He seemed to like his teacher, but I worried over him for a few days. Each day when he would return from school he was scratched and bruised and had his shirttail flying in the breeze. Because of his youth and his curly hair, he was a temptation to the bullies. This noon when he came for luncheon, he was dirty and disheveled, but grinning from ear to ear. "Mama," he said, "there is nothing to it, if you are on the bottom in a fight, all you do is roll over and get on top." I think he will manage.

I made seven pints of Green Tomato pickle yesterday, with the tomatoes we grew in our Victory Garden. It turned out very well. The thing that gives it a good flavor is brown sugar and whole mustard seeds.

Senator Burnet Maybank ate breakfast with us this morning. His wife is still away and he is staying alone in his house. I can't imagine Lister staying here alone and cooking for himself. He can't even boil water.

We had dinner with the Joe Caseys on Sunday night. The party was given for Senator Truman, the Vice Presidential nominee. He plays the piano quite well. The other guests were the Walter Lippmanns and Mrs. Borden Harriman.

Except for being away from home, I like the fall best of any season in Washington. It is the only decent weather we have here. Our maple tree is turning such a beautiful gold.

PART THREE

1943–1950

Ball-Burton-Hatch-Hill

For the last two months I have worked quite a bit on Senate Resolution 114, nicknamed by the press as the B2H2 formula (Ball, Burton, Hatch, Hill). Senate Resolution 114 provides that the United States take the lead in the formation of a United Nations for the peace of the world.

It now appears that we are fighting a losing fight. As far as the resolution itself is concerned, we could lose that phase of the fight without too deep a concern. If the principles within the resolution are lost, then it means the continued annihilation of the human race and a return of the dark ages, if not the complete extermination of all mankind by future wars, for wars there will be unless there is cooperation amongst all nations. I can't help but feel that such a unity is an approach towards the given principles of life. I have never felt a deeper inner satisfaction in being a part of such a movement.

Last night, commentator Dick Harkness of NBC called and asked me to go on his program with Betty Ball to discuss the B2H2 Resolution. The idea is to get all American people to think in terms of a United Nations. Our husbands have gone about the country trying to educate the public, should the war suddenly cease. On the way to the studio I began shaking with utter fright; why had I let myself get into this situation, to speak over a national hookup on radio? Somehow the Lord gives strength when we are in need if we call upon Him—and call upon Him, I did. It worked out all right.

Betty Ball, Selma Burton and I joined our husbands in New York for a meeting to promote their resolution. The three ladies went on Mary Margaret O'Brien's program. This time I was not so terribly nervous, but I don't like public speaking.

A few days later, we had dinner with Bill Bullitt, our former Ambassador to Russia and later our Ambassador to France. Among the company were Mrs. McCloy (wife of the Assistant Secretary of War), and the French Admiral who brought the French fleet to the U.S. and at whose home Francois Darlan was staying when the British captured him. It seem that Darlan's son was dining one night at the home of the Admiral when he was taken gravely ill with polio. The Admiral sent word to Darlan advising him that his son was near unto death and to come at once if he wished to see him again. Darlan came and was captured by the British. Later he decided to aid the British and American troops in the North African invasion. "Darlan," said the Admiral, "had always wished to aid the Allies and had waited for such an opportunity. The French troops in Africa offered little or no resistance to the invaders. Thus, many American lives were saved." In spite of the fact that FDR was severely criticized, it seemed that alliance was a large contributing factor towards the success of the whole North African campaign. Darlan was shortly afterwards shot. This ill-fated gentleman was twice my partner at the dinner table—once at the old Countess' in Brest, France, and again at the French Naval Academy for a luncheon in his home. (This was in 1937 when we toured France with the United States Battle Monuments Commission.)

To go back to the dinner at Ambassador Bullitt's, I was seated on the Ambassador's right. He began the conversation by talking about the S.R. 114, saying he was sorry the resolution had not gotten off to a better start. I replied, "With a better start with whom? If you are referring to the Senate, I agree with you, but if you mean by the people of America, you are greatly mistaken."

The resolution, in his opinion, had failed in the Senate because it did not have the backing of Cordell Hull. Hull and Sumner Welles had not spoken to each other in three years. Hull was away but returned to Washington the day after the resolution was introduced in the Senate. He would therefore have kept his hands off it since Welles encouraged the resolution, and he had not been consulted in the matter. Hull, Bullitt said, was too big a man to be hurt by the slight or oversight, but nevertheless the resolution would have gone over better if it had the backing of the Secretary of State. When Hull spoke, continued Mr. Bullitt, it was as if the American people spoke, because he was so well beloved throughout the country.

I assured him that each of the four Senators sponsoring S.R. 114 had the highest regard for Secretary Hull, but he had been out of town at the time the resolution was brewing. The sponsors had such enthusiastic support from Assistant Secretary of State Welles that it had never occurred to them that he did not represent the views of his chief. Likewise it was Welles who arranged the meeting on Sunday between the President and the four Senators. There was no intentional slight of the Secretary.

Mr. Bullitt replied, "The Senators were just duped. I talked to Burton about the whole affair beforehand and advised him to wait until the Secretary had returned to town, but he did not follow my advice."

"Did you tell Senator Burton of the feud between Hull and Welles?" I asked Mr. Bullitt. His reply was in the negative.

I assured Mr. Bullitt that neither Lister nor I had ever heard one word of gossip concerning a feud between the Secretary and his assistant, and I felt just as certain the other three Senators were just as innocent as we were. I also told him in my opinion the same tragedy that happened after World War I would happen again. The isolationists still were just waiting for a chance to block anything the Executive Branch might have to offer the Democratic and Republican coalition in the Senate.

The four Senators had received between four and five thousand letters from all parts of the country, backing the principles embodied in the Resolution. These letters came from soldiers, soldiers' families, ministers, churches, farmers, industry, labor, writers, women's organizations, and from people in all walks of life. They all expressed gratitude for the four Senators and said, "You seem to be the only ray of hope on an otherwise dark horizon. We pray God for help to come to you in your efforts. We wonder if the people will let us down again as they did after the last war."

It takes an awful lot of praying to do anything constructive for the human race.

It was by then dessert time; the ladies were expected to retire to the living room while the men discussed political matters, a custom I fully dislike. As we were about to depart, I asked one more question: "What are you doing in Washington, Mr. Bullitt? I suppose I ought to know but I don't."

"I am in the Navy Department under Knox," Mr. Bullitt replied.

I knew I should not have said it, but the temptation was too great. "Somehow, I can't quite connect you with the Navy; in my mind you are so closely associated with diplomacy and intrigue."

Days later I heard that Mr. Bullitt had an ulterior motive in telling me of the feud between Welles and Hull. He would like to replace Welles and thus be in a position to succeed Hull in the case the latter should resign because of ill health.

NOVEMBER 1, 1943

Today I sat in the gallery of the Senate and listened to Lister's speech on the Connally Resolution. It has been called a Mother Hubbard—it covers everything but touches nothing. The Senate Foreign Affairs Committee reports that sixteen Senators have decided to fight the Resolution. A lucky break came today, with the announcement of the Moscow Conference, and the acceptance of the four great powers to form a United Nations to preserve the peace after the war. Secretary Hull, who was our representative at Moscow, was given much praise by the Senate body. If the Senators talk on for a few more days until public opinion has time to crystallize, I believe they will demand that the Senate adopt the Moscow Conference report, which is practically embodied by the B2H2. Connally, however, wants to vote immediately.

The publicity campaign that Betty Ball, Rachel Bell, Lillian Coville (now Mrs. Joe Jones) and I put on last spring and summer shows definite results.

Most people know little about the operations of the Congress. Few realize that it takes two-thirds of the Senate to ratify a foreign treaty, and that to sit back and leave it to the Senate and hope for the best is just what happened to the League of Nations. If the Moscow treaty passes, hats off to the trailblazers—the B2H2 boys and Betty Ball's girls. Betty never lost faith in the face of many seeming defeats.

NOVEMBER 18, 1943

This morning I attended a joint session of Congress, at which Cordell Hull, our Secretary of State, reported back to his Government the results of the Moscow Conference. His speech was logical and thoughtful, but his voice was weak, almost to the point of being feeble—time and a heavy workload have begun to tell on him. His reception by Congress was appreciative without being enthusiastic.

On leaving the Chambers, I turned to a friend and asked, "How did he impress you?"

"Full of dignity but completely lacking in appeal," she replied.

Another friend spoke up, "You would think after attending such an inspiring conference, he would have caught something of the fire. To me he has always been a dud, a firecracker that fails to go off. And that is why the American people hold him in such high regard—he seems so safe and sane to them."

Mrs. Hull was dressed in a purplish woolen dress suit on which she had pinned a corsage of deep red roses. She sat on the edge of her seat and seemed exceedingly nervous. I wondered why. As she passed me in the corridor, I overheard someone ask her, "Where was Mrs. Roosevelt today?" Mrs. Hull replied, "I guess she felt this was not an important enough occasion to attend."

The B2H2 Resolution was sent to the Foreign Affairs Committee, of which Senator Tom Connally was the chairman. Here the Connally Bill was written. It contained much of the objectives of the B2H2 resolution. The Connally Bill was passed and a "United Nations" established. While that organization is not all that could be desired, it is at least a beginning.

Fourth and Final Inaugural

Our country was at war, so the fourth Inaugural of FDR was held at the White House rather than on the steps of the Capitol. It snowed most of the night before. The following day was bitter cold and rather grim. Guests for the ceremonies were selected mostly from the Congress, top officials in the Government, cabinet, friends, family, and Supreme Court.

The Supreme Court, cabinet, and family stood on the balcony with the President when he took the oath of office. The rest of the guests stood on a tarpaulin, which covered the wet, soggy ground just below the balcony. FDR wore no hat, but had draped a Navy cape over his shoulders. He looked ghastly.

Our daughter Henrietta, Lister, Lister Jr., Roy Nolen (of Alabama), and I stood close together to view this history-making event. The ceremonies over, we stood in line nearly an hour before getting into the White House. We each had our muddy boots on; there was no place to leave them. History makes mention of the muddy boots at Andrew Jackson's inaugural reception at the White House. There was no parade that day.

The local papers stated that three thousand people were invited to the luncheon and that the food gave out. Ambassador Daniels was reported to have consumed three plates of that awful chicken salad. The salad was mostly celery and each portion a bare spoonful. Served with the salad was a roll, a piece of pound cake and coffee. The food, at such a momentous occasion, was unimportant, but, as Mr. Daniels said to us when we met in the hall, "I was hungry."

The day after the Inauguration I had a talk with Josephine Black who told me that before the oath of office was taken a religious service was held in the White House with the President and his family, the Cabinet, and Members of the Supreme Court with their wives. The President sat in a wheelchair. Immediately following the service, Josephine walked over to the President and tried to speak to him. He seemed preoccupied, so she spoke to him again. "Mr. President," she said, "this is Josephine Black." Still no response. Mrs. Black stood there a few moments. The President stared ahead without seeming to recognize her. In the past he had seemed very fond of her. As the Justice approached, Josephine asked, "Hugo, have you made the President mad at us? He would not speak to me." The Roosevelt family denies that FDR suffered a smaller stroke before his fatal stroke in Warm Springs, Georgia. Josephine was certain in her own mind that he could not speak.

Lister and I entertained at three parties last week. The Sunday night party was the most fun. Senator Happy Chandler, who is an ex-Governor of Kentucky, the Tommie Corcorans, Claude Peppers, the Richard Reynolds (who named the town of Listerhill, Alabama, after Lister), Ben Leader, Tom Beach, and Roy Nolen—the last three from Alabama. Happy Chandler, as the Senator is called, has a beautiful singing voice. At my request Tommie brought along his accordion on which he can play anything. They played and sang until midnight.

The following Thursday we entertained at a farewell party for the Henry Wallaces. With them we had a few of their close friends. Iola took a cocktail, the first I had ever seen her take. She laughed and seemed to relax, and said, "Now I can say anything I want to."

Fortunately for me, we had three turkeys and four wild ducks given to us for Christmas, and which we had put in the deep freeze to be used at our parties during the Inaugural festivities. Otherwise, we could not have managed, with rationing.

Through the Windows

R emember," said Mrs. Angus Dun, the wife of the Episcopal Bishop of Washington, "You are the windows through which these people glimpse the outside world." This she told me as she guided me through the hallways of the Washington Home for Incurables [now St. Elizabeth's Hospital, where John Hinkley is kept]. As the newest member of the Board, I had been asked to serve as a regular visitor. It had not occurred to me that I would be asked to work directly with the patients.

There were some three hundred men, women, and children living at the Home whose cases were in all "probability" incurable—though I was told that a few recovered their health and were able to leave the Home and to resume their former lives.

The doors to the Institution are opened only to those applicants who, after a thorough investigation, prove that they have no other place to go, or no one capable of caring for them. Some pay their own expenses, while a large number make no remuneration whatever.

At the end of my first day as a visitor, I left the Home with the firm determination never to darken its doors again. "I can't take it," I told myself. "Those poor, poor people. I simply can't stand to see them." By the time the following Thursday arrived, the shock has somewhat lessened, and I determined to give the Home one more try. Dressing up in my prettiest and gayest hat and carrying an armful of daffodils I was determined to bring a bit of sunshine to the dreary world of these shut-ins.

The effort was not wasted and I soon found that the patients were not creatures of horror but wonderful friends. In the beginning I suspect that I was given a select few patients to visit; this was to condition me to the Hospital. My first call was to a darling old man, who would have heartily resented the description of "old." He was truly a gentleman of the "old South." When I gave him one of my daffodils, he grasped my hand with his gnarled fingers and said, "I don't know which is the prettiest." He and I fought the "War Between the States" over and over again. The conversation invariably ended with, "The South would have won the war if Richmond had not fallen. They should have kept the Capitol in Montgomery!"

My second call of the day was to William who was a sufferer of Muscular Dystrophy. At the time I made his acquaintance, he had not been out of bed for five years. Before the paralysis was too far advanced, he had been able to pilot himself about the Home in his wheelchair, and had taken his turn at the switchboard. Now he was unable to leave the ancient brass bed that he had brought from his own home. Daily he sat up with a tray across his knees. The tray served as a table for him; on it he kept his tobacco, his pipe, a jar of salve, the radio program, a glass of ice, and a bottle of Pepsi Cola. On a nearby small table sat a radio and the morning papers. We talked about books and travels. The one thing troubling William most was that he felt women were going to the dogs. "History repeats itself," he said one day. "Rome fell when its women became immoral." Then he gravely added, "Women are the backbone of the Nation." Sometimes when I called on him, I found him nodding; I was loathe to waken him, but I knew that he would miss our excursions about the Universe.

I am sure that many times when I visited William, he felt more like crying than smiling, but only twice did he show any inclination to do so. Once I took him a birthday cake. It was an afterthought that occurred to me on my way to the Hospital. The only cake I could find was a lopsided chocolate cake from the bakery shop. "I never had a birthday cake before," he said. There were tears in his eyes, though the words "Thank you" were lost some place way down in his throat. Because of my embarrassment (and to break the silence), I suggested that he blow out the candles and make a wish. With one puff he extinguished all of the candles except one. Disgustedly he said, "Now it won't come true, and I wished that you would never miss a Thursday coming to see me." Of all the things he might have wished, I was touched. The only other time I ever saw him cry was the day I told him that I was being transferred to another wing of the hospital. "It can't be true," he said. He was inconsolable. I had to promise to stop by to say hello on each visit.

I did not venture to tell any of the other patients I was being transferred. Perhaps it was just as well that the transfer came when it did, for then the patients would have a brand new audience to listen to their troubles, and a different point of view of that world of which they were no longer a part.

I could just imagine the gleam in the eyes of my one Indian patient when he discovered that my replacement was the wife of Supreme Court Justice Harold Burton. My Indian friend held an old Indian Claim against the Government for $300,000, which the courts had rejected several times. In spite of the fact that he was well past eighty, the thought that he might one day win his suit, kept him alive. I had been warned in the beginning not to let him know that my husband was connected with the Government, but sly old fox that he was, he found out some way. It didn't take him long to employ me in writing letters to Congressional Committees and to all sorts of people. We had about exhausted all his resources when I was transferred.

My new assignment took me through the entire East Wing of the building. In No. 37, I found a man who could not speak, for he had no vocal cords, but he took my hand and smiled when I told him that spring would soon be here and then he would be able to see the lovely Forsythia blooming from his window.

The curly-haired lad next door spoke only occasionally, though his eyes lit up when you wound a mechanical toy that started two miniature boxers fighting. His neighbor in No. 39 was known as the laughing boy. He hadn't a care in the world. He could not speak, but he could laugh and laugh until he tore your heart to shreds, and you wept if you let yourself.

Across the hall from these unfortunate youths lived an ex-Congressman, who spent most of his time in his wheelchair, visiting around the building and dreaming of past glories. At my request, Lister sent him the "Congressional Record." From then on, we spent our time together discussing the issues of the day. Sometimes we agreed, sometimes not. One day, he was in a fury. He had just finished reading the proceedings of the day before; the Senate had tried to deny Senator Bilbo of Mississippi a seat in the Senate. "To deny Bilbo interferes with States Rights. Mississippi elected him and the Senate has no right to throw him out," he shouted.

Perhaps the patient who caused me the most concern occupied No. 41. He was a tax expert, a highly intelligent man, and an excellent musician. He was always studying, reading, or listening to symphonies on the radio. His too-active mind and too-sensitive nature filled him with resentment against the tragic accident that had condemned him to a life of inactivity in a world of "Shut Ins." When summer came, he had his bed moved to the screened porch where he spent many hours sunning himself, in the hope that the God-given rays would heal his malady, while I in turn prayed that the Great Physician would heal the soul of this embittered man.

No story is quite complete without a bit of romance. In the late spring I acquired a new patient, a handsome young man with a roguish grin. When he smiled, which he did frequently, he displayed glistening white teeth. Beneath his bed sat a bottle with a tube inside, while the other end of the tube was inserted somewhere within his body. His life's history is too tragic to relate in full. Pneumonia at eighteen months, run over by a horse and buggy at age six (resulting in a fractured skull), father died at fourteen, then an unsuccessful marriage, a series of jobs and operations. In spite of all his woes he continued to smile and to display a remarkable resilience. That smile eventually captured the heart of one of the nurses in the hospital; they were married and she took him home to care for him. They were both confident that now he would get well.

I made a point of saving my last visit of the day for George, the brother of William, the sufferer of Muscular Dystrophy. I was glad that he was the last on my list for he both amused and entertained me. George had already been in the Home for six years when William was admitted. The two brothers were as different as night from day, excepting they were both victims of a muscular deterioration. "Congenital," said George. The other patients referred to George as the "King Fish."

There would have been no need for me to call upon George before twelve o'clock; he slept until ten. If I arrived too early, he was apt to be shaving or being dressed by his nurse. Because of his great bulk and his infirmity, George had designed for himself a rather picturesque costume— a garment both practical and comfortable. It consisted of a loose satin blouse with large sleeves gathered into a tight band at the wrists; with it he wore black satin pajama pants. To vary the costume, in summer he wore short sleeved blouses in outlandish colors.

George had brought his own furniture with him to the Home. In one corner sat a large red leather chair; there was also a chest of drawers and an oversized mahogany desk. The walls of the room were filled with paintings—all copies of the old masters, and photographs of actresses and actors.

Day in and day out, the King Fish sat in his wheelchair before the desk with all the dignity of a too well fed affluent executive. He had a private telephone installed; this kept him in touch with the outside world—as he told me he was a man of influence, with outside connections. Through his influence with the Variety Club, the Home had received a donation of a movie projector and weekly movies for the patients. As soon as all the equipment was paid for, George started on another project, a dental clinic. Not until he suffered a toothache himself was he aware that the Home had no facilities for giving dental care to the patients. Some weeks later he chuckled like a boy when he told me that he had secured a dental chair and an electric drill for the Home.

The King Fish always kept his door closed; he liked his privacy but when I knocked on his door, he called, "Come in, Mrs. Hill," and in the intonation of his voice I could detect not a note of arrogance but of defiance of the disease he knew would one day possess him. "Troubles," said George. "Everybody has troubles. Who wants to listen to other people's troubles?"

I was always tired when I left the Home for the Incurables. I had given a lot of myself when I was there, but those people had given me far more than I ever gave them. If I brought them a bit of sunshine and a peek at the outside world, they in return showed me how to live life without a hope and to live it courageously.

Politics, Protocol, & People

Lister's brother, Luther Hill, came to dinner one night for a little family get-together. L.L. (as he was known) was a graduate of West Point but had resigned his commission and gone to work for Cowles Publications in Des Moines, Iowa. When war broke out, he volunteered to reenter the service. He was given the rank of General and assigned to the Pentagon.

After our dinner, we were sitting around in the living room chatting when L.L. said, "What I am going to tell you must be held in utmost secrecy. You must not tell anyone what you are about to hear. We have the most powerful bomb in the world. It is so powerful, it will end the war with Japan."

(We didn't know it at the time, but what he was talking about was the atomic bomb, which ultimately we dropped on Hiroshima and Nagasaki, ending World War II.)

SPRING 1945

This noon I went to the Capitol to a luncheon that Senator and Mrs. John Bankhead gave for his niece, Tallulah Bankhead. All of the Alabama delegation was there. It was really a lovely party. After the luncheon, Lister was called on to make a speech; it went something like this: "Massachusetts has its Adams family, Virginia has its Lee family, and Alabama has its Bankhead family . . ." Tallulah then got up and replied in her very best play-acting style. After she had called everybody *Darling*, she went over to a bust of her father, Will Bankhead, a former Speaker of the House, threw her arms around the neck of the statue and gave it a lingering smack on the lips.

Last night we attended a party at the Joe Davies'. Mrs. Davies owns Post Cereals and is one of the wealthiest women in the world. She owns "Tregaron," the most beautiful house in Washington. There were thirty guests for the dinner, all seated at the same table, with one butler for every four persons.

The table was covered with a gold cloth with real lace placemats for everyone. There were gold service plates, gold candelabras, gold cutlery, and a gold epergne filled with Calla lilies (about $75 worth). It was the most elegant affair I have ever attended.

For the first course we were served Russian caviar with a small glass of Vodka. Since I had never tasted Vodka, I turned to my dinner partner and asked, "Do you sip Vodka?" Whereupon he explained that you were supposed to just toss it off in one big gulp. Then I started to tell him about Mexico and seeing the natives suck a lemon and then toss back a glass of tequila, which was supposed to be as strong as Vodka. He interrupted me to say, "Excuse me, but I must talk to the lady on my left first as she outranks you. I will get back to you later." Right then and there I put him down as suffering from what I call "Protocolic." It is a common disease in Washington.

We had coffee and liqueurs in the drawing room, after which we were taken into the sun parlor to see the movie *A Song to Remember* about the life of Chopin. The music in the picture is played by Iturbi, one of today's greatest pianists.

I am invited back to "Tregaron" tomorrow for a reception Mrs. Davies is giving for Mrs. Roosevelt, Madam Wei Tao Ming (the Chinese Ambassador's wife), Madame Gromyko (the Russian Ambassador's wife), Madam Bonnet (the French Ambassador's wife), Mrs. Stettinius (wife of the Secretary of State), and Lady Sanson. That is quite an outlay, isn't it?

We are expecting another snow tomorrow. No signs of spring yet though I did see a robin today.

APRIL 12, 1945
SPRING VALLEY

It was a beautiful sunny day; the azaleas were in bloom and were a riot of color. I had been invited to a tea at Mrs. Harry Hawes, just around the corner on Quebec Street. The distance was so short I walked to the party. Mrs. Hawes is wife of Missouri's U.S. Senator. I had only been at the party for ten minutes when someone asked me if I had heard of FDR's death in Warm Springs, Georgia. It had been announced over the radio. We guests began to trickle away.

Lister was at that very minute on his way to Louisville, Kentucky to make a speech the following day (Jefferson's birthday). His train had left the station only ten minutes before. All the way home I kept asking myself what I could do. I was certain all the Jefferson Day dinners would be cancelled. When I reached home, I grabbed for the telephone and called the Station Master in Alexandria to ask if the train had left. It was just pulling into the station. I asked the Station Master to try to give Lister my message. Unfortunately, the Station Master gave the message to the Conductor, who gave it to Lister after the train left Alexandria. So Lister continued on to Charlottesville before he could detrain. In the wee small hours I heard a car door slam. It was Lister coming home.

APRIL 13, 1945

President Roosevelt's body arrived this morning from Georgia. The body will lie in state in the East Room at the White House. I did not go in town with Lister this morning to see the funeral procession. Those who did see the procession said it was the most solemn occasion they ever witnessed. The streets were jammed with weeping people who came to pay their respects to a man who called them "My Friends."

Lister is going to Hyde Park for the funeral. Because of space, no wives will be allowed.

OCTOBER 8, 1945

Lister took Junior down to see the Nimitz parade today, but I was tired and did not try to go. I listened to the radio and watched the planes overhead. There were a thousand planes in the air at one time. They flew in formation making the word NIMITZ. It was a spectacular sight.

LAST NIGHT I WENT to the White House and took Henrietta to an entertainment that the Senate Ladies sponsored for two hundred wounded soldiers from the local hospitals. Our daughters entertained the young men, and the Senate Ladies waited on the tables. After supper, there was dancing for the boys who were able. Many were legless, however, and had crutches or were in wheelchairs. One amputee did an exhibition dance with a nurse. I think the boys really got a kick out of being at the party.

Tonight we are invited to a dinner for the new Secretary of War, Robert Patterson. He is an old friend of ours, and quite a nice person.

Tuesday night we had Mr. Alfred Knopf, the publisher, for dinner with a few other friends, including the Mervin Sterns of Birmingham. Wednesday night we dined at the Wallaces, along with the three top scientists who worked on the atomic bomb. One was from Westinghouse, one a Hungarian, and the third a German. I can't spell any of their names. Unfortunately, it was a discussion meeting and all the men went into the library while the wives sat and chitchatted. I was dying to hear what the men had to say, but had no choice.

Tomorrow night we go to Senator Brian McMahon's birthday party. We were invited out on Sunday night, but we declined as we thought we would be too tired by then.

My new dinner dress arrived this afternoon, but if this social whirl doesn't let up I will have to buy another one.

MAY 1946

One afternoon I lunched with Mrs. James M. Helm in her apartment on Connecticut Avenue. Mrs. Helm was Social Secretary at the White House during the Roosevelt Administration, and now is serving in the same capacity for the Truman Administration. Invitations were out for the annual Senate Ladies Red Cross luncheon, with Mrs. Truman and the Cabinet wives as hostesses. Mrs. Helm and I were discussing the recent redecorations of the family quarters at the White House. (This was a year or so before the Trumans suddenly realized that the floors had begun to sink and the White House was slowly deteriorating.) As I was talking to Mrs. Helm, I had what I thought was a brilliant idea. "Do you suppose that Mrs. Truman would let the Senate Ladies make a tour of the White House family quarters when we come there for the Red Cross luncheon next Tuesday?"

"I can't say," Mrs. Helm replied, "but I will deliver your message to Mrs. Truman."

The day of the luncheon turned out to be beautiful and sunny. Chairs and tables were scattered about beneath the trees on the White House lawn, with the red-coated Marine band playing in the background. A delicious buffet was being served to the guests. I had just begun to wonder if we were going to be invited on a tour of the White House living quarters when Mrs. Truman walked over to the table where I was sitting and asked, "Mrs. Hill, you don't think any of the ladies would care to tour the upstairs of the White House, do you?"

"Yes, I do," I said hopefully. "Very few of them have ever visited the upstairs." The ladies were thrilled when they heard the news. Few if any failed to accept.

The living quarters of the first family had a comfortable homelike atmosphere. The walls were freshly painted; new chintz curtains hung at the windows and new slipcovers covered most of the chairs.

I had only once visited the upstairs of the White House. That was the time we dined with the President and Mrs. Roosevelt and were taken upstairs to view a movie, *The Philadelphia Story*, which was shown on a screen set up in the hall. That night we were not invited to see any of the upstairs rooms.

When Mrs. Truman piloted us through the living quarters, I was shocked to find out that there were so few bathrooms and a dearth of closets. Mrs. Truman hung her clothes in a cupboard. With the exception of the rooms of the first family, the other bedrooms were grossly inadequate for our President and his family and guests. There was almost a total lack of fine furniture. It was surprising to see some of the rooms furnished with iron beds and painted furniture.

Soon after our tour, the floors in the White House were discovered sinking beneath Margaret's piano, and the walls disintegrating. The first family quickly moved across the street to the Blair Lee House, which is owned by the Government and used to house official guests. It was while the Trumans were living here that the President was shot at by a Puerto Rican—one of the policemen was killed guarding our President.

A surprising number of political pros around Washington make the same assessment of Harry S. Truman: "History will record Harry Truman as a great President, a man of integrity and exceptional courage." No president has been called upon to make as many tough decisions. The decision to drop the atom bomb must have cost him many a sleepless night. To relieve General Douglas MacArthur (a national hero) of his command in Korea, the Berlin Airlift, and the Truman Doctrine for Greece and Turkey saved many lives. Our President let the world know the "Man of Independence" could not be pushed around.

APRIL 1949

This afternoon I attended a reception at the Congressional Club, which was given by Justice and Mrs. Harold Burton of the Supreme Court. President Truman was mingling among the guests. Now was the time, I thought, to avail myself of an opportunity I had longed for ever since Josephus Daniels died January 19, 1948, and so it was that I told Mr. Truman of my last ride with Mr. Daniels.

Mr. Daniels had visited Washington last spring, just at Cherry Blossom time. He had called our house and learned that I was attending a Board meeting and luncheon for the "Society of Sponsors" at the Mayflower Hotel.

After the meeting, when I came out of the hotel, there was Mr. Daniels waiting for me at the door. "I have a White House car waiting for me and I want you to go someplace with me," he said. We got into the waiting limousine, then he instructed the chauffeur to take us for a drive around the Speed Way, to see the cherry blossoms blooming there.

After our ride, Mr. Daniels directed the driver to take us to the Jefferson Memorial. Upon our arrival, we got out of the car and climbed the marble steps to the Memorial that houses a giant statue of Thomas Jefferson. We viewed the statue for a moment, then descended a pair of back stairs leading to the basement. "I wanted to see how much space is beneath the rotunda. I think Thomas Jefferson was our greatest President and I would like to convert all of this waste space into a research library, so that anyone wishing to make a study of his life and works could come here and do so. I would collect all his portraits, all his writings and all the things written about him, and place them here for students. People come here and look at the statue and go away not knowing of the greatness of the man. I hope some day this will be done."

I couldn't help thinking, *Mr. Daniels wants me to remember what he is saying, in case anything happens to him.* He looked so feeble that afternoon my heart was saddened. When he returned me to the Mayflower parking lot, he bent over and kissed me goodbye. I think in his heart, he knew it was farewell.

I am sorry to say Mr. Truman did not seem the least bit interested in the Jeffersonian Library at the time. But I hope someday that someone in power will catch the vision of Mr. Daniels. A monument to a great man is an inspiration in itself—think how much more important is the preservation of the essence of his greatness. It is the spirit of a man that stirs other men's blood.

Lister and I shall always miss Mr. Daniels. He was a grand old man whose friendship enriched our lives.

Cornelia Was Quite a Girl

Cornelia is one of the most vivid and interesting personalities I have ever known. Really, she is quite a girl! Allow me to present to you Mrs. Gifford Pinchot, whose given name is Cornelia. (Her husband served two terms as Governor of Pennsylvania.)

Cornelia does not belong to that vast group of the living dead who stalk the streets. She is a rare soul, who is vitally interested in life and in every living creature. Born with a silver spoon in her mouth, with a long line of distinguished ancestors, she has nevertheless had a keen interest in people and in politics. At twenty, Cornelia was a great beauty with Titian hair. At middle age, as the wife of the Governor of Pennsylvania, she was still a beautiful woman, more interested, however, in probing into coalmines and trying to better the living conditions of the workers than in attending tea parties.

Now at an indeterminate age ranging somewhere between sixty-five and seventy-five (when most of her contemporaries are reminiscing), Cornelia is still quite a girl. Life, for or with Cornelia, is never dull. Though faded with the years, she is still striking in appearance. Her hair, which by all laws of nature should be snow white, is a Valentine pink, and is worn in the style of the Gay Nineties. Before anyone takes a second stare at her unnatural coiffure, she startles them with, "You know I dye my hair." Not that this statement is at all necessary, but such absolute frankness does give one a start and you feel like saying, "I would never have suspected it."

In dress, Cornelia runs to the exotic. Her color combinations are often exquisite and express her personality—a youthful spirit that refuses to be conquered, though imprisoned by age.

I saw Cornelia at a dinner at the Harlan F. Stones' home a few years ago. She was wearing a gold lamé dress of five seasons past. When she walked into the drawing room, I gasped to myself at the changes she had rendered in her costume. At the neckline was pinned a bit of real lace. Around her throat she wore great chunks of green glass beads entwined with a long string of pearls. Trailing from her waist were pink roses and ivy, which hung almost to the hem of her gown.

When dinner was over and the guests were filing out of the dining room, I overheard Mrs. Stone remark to Mrs. Pinchot, "What an unusual costume you have on tonight."

Mrs. Stone (who is ultra conservative in dress) and I were probably thinking the same thing about Mrs. Pinchot's outfit. Whatever Mrs. Stone's thoughts were, I am sure she did not expect the reply she received. "You can't press this material," Cornelia said, "and I thought tonight as I put on this old dress that it looked exactly as if I had slept in it; so I did the best I could to cover it up. The roses came off an old hat and the ivy was yanked off one of the columns in my dining room."

The columns of which she spoke have always intrigued me. They are only six feet tall and lack five feet of reaching the ceiling. There are six of them placed nonchalantly about the spacious dining room. Cornelia took a fancy to them and transported them all the way from some ancient ruins in Italy. They have been strung with wires and made useful by Cornelia's ingeniousness. In the top of the columns are concealed electric lights which throw a luminous glow around the room and over her perfectly appointed dinners, which are worthy of a poet. They should be set down in lyrics to be sung by future bards. I have met there the most interesting people in Washington, ranging from the Chief Justice of the Supreme Court, Cabinet members, Senators, Ambassadors, business executives, labor leaders, and almost all celebrities in the Nation's capital.

Cornelia's table decorations are always colorful and artistic. Any Garden Club member, who is an aspirant for a club prize, could learn a great deal from her arrangements. On one occasion I recall a large, old-fashioned compote containing nearly everything in the market at that season, such as peppers, squash, artichokes, great clusters of green and purple grapes, apples, and pears.

For dinner there is apt to be pheasant, and the platter is invariably decorated at one end with a pheasant's head and at the other with the tail feathers from this colorful bird. Likely as not the dessert will be "Smokey Joe," a baked Alaska built up like a volcano from which great columns of smoke erupt. No intoxicating beverages are ever served by the hostess, but the cuisine is unsurpassed.

After dinner the guests wander into the drawing room. This room runs the full length of the house and must be more than sixty feet long and about a third as wide. A cheerful log fire crackles on the hearth, while an ancient Great Dane on wobbly legs flounders around. Bookcases line the walls and are filled with many well-worn books. Here you will find curios collected from the four corners of the earth: a Chinese jade horse, ancient Greek urns, and rare antique furniture. Here is culture and charm and a warmth of friendship to be shared with all.

Most of Cornelia's gatherings have been for a cause. The last party I attended at the Pinchots' was given in honor of the atomic scientists, shortly after the bombing of Hiroshima. These scientists, overcome by a feeling of tremendous responsibility to civilization, came to Washington to try to impress the "powers that be" with the destructibility of the monster that they had created. Our hostess, herself an acutely aware person, sought to bring together in her home a group of people she felt could assist these men in their effort to control the use of the atomic bomb.

At another time, I attended a committee meeting at the Pinchots' home, with a group of women who were interested in the formation of a United Nations organization. On this occasion I was summoned to the telephone in Cornelia's bedroom, and I must say I was not quite prepared for Cornelia's own sanctuary. On reflection, it was again typical of her—surprising, audacious, and yet completely unpretentious. The door was painted an electric blue. For extra light, she had cut out stars and a Turkish crescent in the top portion of her door. The room itself could not have been more than eight by ten. Its furnishings consisted of a chest, a bed, and a chair. This was all that the occupant felt that she needed for her personal use.

During the early days of the war I invited Cornelia to a small dinner. The Governor, whose health had begun to fail, could not come, so she came alone, arriving about an hour late. She was dressed this time in her blue Office of Civilian Defense uniform. Everyone else was in evening clothes, but this did not disturb her in the least. She had worked hard and late at her job in the OCD, and had not found time to change.

One of the guests asked Mrs. Pinchot what she was doing for the war effort. She surprised them with her answer: "I have just finished making a survey of the town for possible space for the homeless in case of bombings. When we are bombed, I will be on hand to feed you onion soup and to see that you get to a hospital in a hurry."

I don't doubt at all that Cornelia would have made good her promise, if such a need had arisen in the City of Washington.

All during the war I read of Cornelia's many activities for the war effort. Now and then our paths crossed as we served on different committees together. It seemed to me that she was expending more energy than was necessary for one who might easily have joined the sock knitters—but Cornelia seemed to thrive on activity.

Early in the fall when I learned that Governor Pinchot had died, I wondered what would become of Cornelia. Theirs had been such a beautiful partnership of service to their fellow man. Would she sit now by the fireside, alone with her grief? The answer came this morning, in the paper, in the form of an announcement of a meeting to be held at her home, for the board members of "America United for World Government."

So—Cornelia is still concerned with the future; she has no time for herself or the past. Such people never really grow old.

Glamour
[Written for a now-unknown "Labor" magazine.]

Life as a Senator's wife is a broadening experience, full of excitement, interesting people—and, I may add, many trials and tribulations. Long ago, however, I found that for anything worthwhile, you pay a price.

I believe the greatest satisfaction a Senator's wife can find is in the feeling that she has been of help to her husband in serving the people he represents. Perhaps the part I have enjoyed most, as a Senator's wife, is the people I have known. It has been my observation that all people, from the highest station to the lowest position, have something to give if we have open minds and hearts.

The most stimulating personality I have known on the Washington scene was Franklin Roosevelt. I shall never forget the thunderous applause which greeted him when he arose to address a joint session of Congress the day after Pearl Harbor. "Yesterday," he began, "was a day which shall live in infamy." Somehow he gave that vast, bewildered crowd faith and courage.

Then there was another joint session of Congress, addressed by Winston Churchill. He charmed us with the magic of his words and made us feel that he was one of us with, "If my mother had been born in England instead of my father, and father in America instead of my mother, I might have got here on my own" (as a Member of the Congress).

Soon afterwards there was Madam Chiang Kai-shek who held the Congress spellbound with her grace of movement and her soft Southern accent acquired at Wesleyan College. She was a never-to-be-forgotten figure, clad in a simple black Chinese robe, pleading for aid for her countrymen.

Then I remember the Queen of England dressed in a pink tulle evening gown, all shining and dewy with rhinestones, but with a real diamond tiara on her head—looking every bit like a story book queen.

There was another day when the Duke and "the woman I love" sat in the Senate Gallery like any other tourists—but not for long, for someone discovered them and the Congress rose in a body to applaud.

I have told you only of the great or near great, for I found long ago that everyone expects "glamour" from Washington. They do not always stop to think that a Senator's wife has all the household duties of other women, children to raise, PTA meetings to attend, Red Cross work to do, mending and darning—on top of the many demands made upon her as an official hostess. She acts as an unpaid secretary for her husband's many business calls to their home, and many callers. She reads her husband's speeches and offers suggestions. Then there are the last-minute guests her husband brings to dinner to discuss legislation or personal matters. (Some day I'm going to write a cookbook on how to serve eight with a dinner for four. Our fourteen-year-old-son has often complained about his watered soup—and our cocker spaniel has been unhappy over the few scraps left.)

Our daughter Henrietta will graduate from college with a major in government because, she said, "I felt it would make me a better citizen." Secretly, I think she is interested in politics.

I wish more women were interested in politics. Perhaps it would be a better world and we wouldn't be wondering now, "Are we headed for World War III?" It seems to me that this would be an excellent time for all women to gather together in their committees and meetings and do a lot of praying.

So you see, there are many things on my mind these days besides parties, ambassadors, and the usual Washington glamour pictured by the average columnist.

PART FOUR

1951–1959

Cruising the Mediterranean

L ister, his brother, General Luther "L. L." Hill, his wife Mary, and I sailed on the *Escambia* for a Mediterranean cruise in October of 1951. (It was not a junket, for as Lister said, "Mr. Hill paid the freight himself.") We were welcomed on board ship by several of the company's officials, who directed us to our flower-filled suite. These men advised us that there was a strike threatened, which could prevent our ship from sailing. Finally an arrangement was made whereby the officials cut the ropes themselves, letting the *Escambia* slip slowly away.

A few miles down the river, we had a rendezvous with our ship's Captain, who met us in a launch and came aboard. The officials then climbed into the launch and returned to shore. We were soon out to sea.

The ocean was calm and beautiful. We sat in our deck chairs soaking up the sun and letting the waves wash away our tension.

In a short while we knew most of the passengers. They were all friendly, and all were in a holiday mood, except a group of Mormons who were traveling together, with their Minister, to the Middle East. The Mormon religion requires each of their members to spend two years in some kind of welfare work. The leader of the group had organized the party, bringing many from his congregation with him. The group was composed of a minister, technicians, veterinarians, agronomists, and men of many skills.

The night before they were to disembark, some of the women became apprehensive. They were not certain what lay in store for them and their families. The Minister came to Lister and asked him to talk to his group to try to help restore their confidence in themselves and in their mission. Shortly after dinner, Lister and I attended a meeting of the Mormons in the lounge. This was an extremely delicate situation, since no one knew what lay ahead. Lister told them that they were new pioneers and would act as goodwill ambassadors who could do more for the peace of the world than any group he knew. Then we bid these courageous people good luck and goodbye.

I have often wondered how they survived, with the many hardships they must have had to face in a strange country, hearing a strange tongue spoken.

BARCELONA, SPAIN

Our first port of call was Barcelona, Spain. The ship anchored in the harbor two days and a night. We slept on the ship, going ashore to sightsee during the day. Most of the people we saw looked both poor and unhappy. The majority of the women wore black, as quite a few were in mourning.

We toured the city and shopped a bit, buying a few presents for the family. It was not the bullfighting season, but we were shown the arena where the fights took place. Our guide then took us to view the bulls in their pens. Next we visited the Chapel. Here the matadors and toreadors came to pray before entering the ring. Adjoining the Chapel was a fully equipped hospital room, just in case the bull won the argument. I am not sure I could sit through a bullfight, though I have been told that bullfighters spend a lifetime in training. Some of them are graceful as ballerinas, and their performances are sheer artistry.

MARSEILLES, FRANCE

In Marseilles, France, the next port we visited, we were only allowed two days ashore. Our guide suggested that we might drive inland for a change, to see Avignon, the city of the Popes, only a short distance from Marseilles. We decided to take his advice and make the Pilgrimage. The Palace is said to be a masterpiece of 14th century Gothic work. From 1309 to 1377 Avignon was a Papal seat. We found the Palace most interesting.

All along the highway, we drove through acres of olive trees, some of them centuries old. The second day in Marseilles, we toured the waterfront, driving down a portion of the French Riviera. It was too cold for bikinis or beach parties, but sailboats were still in evidence. It had been a delightful day.

We hated to say goodbye to France, but the ship was about to sail away, bound for Naples, Italy. Naples has everything—opera, magnificent homes, mountains, poverty, and a beautiful harbor. We particularly enjoyed our trip to Sorrento and Salerno, where our American soldiers climbed the perilous beaches over rocks and crags to capture a foothold in Italy.

On the return trip to Naples, the guide took us by way of the Amalfi Drive. The road is narrow and winding, and our chauffeur took us around the curves at breakneck speed. We enjoyed the ride in spite of him.

Most of the Amalfi Drive is along the Mediterranean. Up and down the mountainside, we saw farmers tending their grape arbors. The terracing of the mountain must have taken backbreaking labor to prepare such rocky soil for cultivation.

I wish we had allowed more time to see the ruins of Pompeii. As a child I used to look at *Stoddard's Lectures* and was fascinated by the story of Pompeii. It was amazing to find how many articles that had been excavated could still be useful today.

ALEXANDRIA, EGYPT

The night before we were to land in the Port of Alexandria, Lister and I retired rather early. Along about eleven o'clock we heard voices outside. Someone rapped on the window, calling us to come out—we were being serenaded. In a very few minutes we were dressed and joined the crowd. A dear little French woman whose husband worked for the State Department had organized these people.

Each participant sang, danced, or played a musical instrument. Some came as listeners. There were many nationalities represented in the group. Here we were all one family, and there was no language barrier. This was a lovely thing for these people to do for us.

When I looked out the window next morning, what I saw could easily have been a Hollywood movie set. This was Africa. There were Fezes, camels, monkeys, vendors, noise and heat.

The American Consul, Mr. Wright, met our party. He came aboard to welcome us, and to call on Lister. He then presented us with an invitation to a dinner from our Ambassador, Jefferson Caffrey. The dinner was to be held in the American Embassy in Cairo.

Having welcomed us officially, Consul Wright then gave us the run down on the situation in Egypt, which was very tense. The third Secretary at the Embassy in Cairo had been slain only a few days before. Consul Wright told us that while Ambassador Caffrey would be happy to see us and to give the dinner should we decide to visit Cairo, he (Mr. Wright) felt that the Ambassador would be relieved not to have the responsibility of a Senator visiting in Cairo under the circumstances. Consul Wright added that he wished we would think the matter over, and if we decided to remain in Alexandria, the Wrights would like to give a small dinner for us in their home. He hoped to make our visit in Alexandria both interesting and enjoyable.

Cairo was one of the places we most wanted to see. We were terribly disappointed not to see the pyramids. After a short discussion we concluded that we would not run the risk of a possible incident or encounter. Also, our presence would be a burden on the Ambassador—so we four Hills stayed in Alexandria and had a lovely time; all thanks to the Wrights.

The Wrights invited most of the local officials, and a few friends to dinner and to meet us. The next day, the Commissioner of Agriculture entertained in our honor at a luncheon in his desert home. I guess my vision of a desert home, and a desert, was based entirely on Hollywood— that is, nothing but miles and miles of beautiful white sand, and a silken tent as a home. Deeper in the desert there may be white sand, but what we saw looked like the black soil of Alabama! The home of the Commissioner was not a silken tent, just a brick bungalow with all the modern conveniences.

After a most enjoyable luncheon, the Commissioner invited all his guests to see his experimental garden. He held the theory that Africa was full of underground springs, and these springs could be uncovered if you dug deep enough. The soil was rich and productive. If you added water, you could grow anything. The entire garden was well irrigated. There were peach and fig trees and a variety of vegetables, and flowers of all kinds. It was exciting.

Alexandria is a beautiful, modern city with quite a few lovely homes. We left feeling very grateful for all the Wrights did for our pleasure.

LEBANON

At last we reached Lebanon. As we were about to go down for breakfast, there was a rap on our door. It was Consul Wynn Lyon from the American Embassy, who wished to take us ashore immediately. The Arab world was in turmoil, and the Ambassador was afraid that the Lebanese might decide to put on a sympathetic demonstration in spite of the fact that they were our friends. In a little less than a half hour the General, Mary, Lister, and I were off the ship and speeding to our hotel. As soon as we were housed and out of the way of possible incidents, we ordered breakfast sent up to the room. Consul Lyon informed us that we were not to leave the room until he called. In the meantime our door was to be locked to everyone. First Egypt, and now Lebanon. These demonstrations were danger signals that the Arab countries were in an angry mood.

Around three o'clock we received a telephone call from Mr. Lyon saying they felt we were now reasonably safe. There appeared to be no sign of a demonstration, and he would call for us at four o'clock to take us for a ride around the city of Beirut. Lebanon was a far more beautiful country than I had realized.

We dined that night with the Ambassador in the Embassy. The next day we went sightseeing, ending at the American University for tea. Dr. Steven B.L. Penrose was President of the University at that time. He and his wife are a charming couple. We discussed many things, mostly the unrest of the Arab nations.

The next day we drove out to see the Arab refugee encampments. The first group we visited was housed in an old church. Each family occupied a small cubicle, separated from his neighbor by a rug, a blanket, or anything he could get to hang on ropes or poles, to make a crude tent. Each occupant was allowed lying down room only. We visited several more of these camps; the others we saw were not as congested, but everyone lived in tents. It was easy to see why these Arabs were unhappy over their situation. The children ran after us crying "Buckskins" (money).

The following day we drove to Baalbek to see the gigantic ancient ruins of the marble temples. They are almost as beautiful and as interesting as the ruins of the Acropolis in Greece, though not as well known. Baalbek is one of the oldest cities in Lebanon. In the beginning of its era it was a small village with a temple erected to Hadad, the Sun God. Baalbek received much attention from its conquerors. First the Greeks, then the Romans and Byzantines took Baalbek. I was tempted to mount a camel to have a picture made—but Mr. Lyon said they were covered with fleas.

The Holy Land

While we were eating breakfast the next morning, I inquired, "Why the guards around our room last night?" then it came out. We were the first guests to occupy the new suite since it was rebuilt. The State Department had sent George McGhee on a special mission to Damascus. The day after McGhee had departed, the wing of the Embassy in which he had been staying was dynamited, destroying the entire wing. Now we understood why we were not permitted to stay at a hotel.

Our substitute host took very good care of us. He gave us an interesting tour of the city, both modern and ancient. I was told that the bazaar in Cairo was quite similar to the bazaar in Damascus. (I purchased one of the large tin-on-copper trays. It sits in our living room today. We use it for a coffee table.)

Upon our return to Beirut, Lister and I packed our bags and sent them back to the *Escambia*, as we had plans to fly to Jerusalem, taking with us only one bag each. We were to rejoin the passengers on the *Escambia* when the ship docked in Greece.

We left Beirut in a small cabin plane, accompanied by a very nice couple from Colorado. We later learned that our plane had been nicknamed "The Orange Crate." It was one of the American discards after

World War II. We were totally unaware that the airport officials had fired every red flare they had to signal our pilot to return to the field. Weather reports had come in a few minutes after takeoff: the Jerusalem airport was completely shut down because of rain and fog. We went gaily on.

Our pilot knew his Biblical history. He swooped down to give us a closer view of the Sea of Galilee. Then he circled a Crusader's Castle. The mountains we crossed were so barren I wondered how sheep or camels or anything could subsist on that wasteland.

Finally the pilot received a message that we were to land in Arman, Jordan, as the airport in Jerusalem was closed in. This was a blow to us. Fortunately our traveling companions had engaged a car with a guide to meet them at the airport. They invited us to share their car and expenses for the tour. We were overjoyed to accept their offer, as we were fifty miles from Jerusalem.

The four of us lunched in Arman. Our guide told us that since we were so close to our destination, he had worked out a plan whereby we could do the tour of the Holy Land backwards.

We began our tour at the Dead Sea. Lister has never ceased to kid me for stepping into the briny waters. I was so entranced in watching the golden sunset that I backed into the water. The salt on my shoes would never come out.

In Jericho we saw a portion of the famous wall, which had surrounded the city. Our guide told us his version of the fall of the city. This was one I had never heard before. Each time the soldiers marched around the city they drove a stick into the wall. On the seventh trip the trumpets sounded as a signal to ignite the sticks, and because of the terrific heat, the walls crumbled. I am sure they are many versions of the famous incident.

On reaching the Jordan River we found the weather to be wet and rainy. We decided against climbing down the slippery banks of the world's most celebrated stream. Instead we viewed the Jordan from a bridge that crosses the river. The Jordan flows southward through the Holy Land for one hundred fifty eight miles. It is a narrow stream, looking more like a creek than a river.

Christ was baptized here in the Jordan. He preached here to the multitudes, feeding five thousand people with two fishes and five loaves of bread.

Towards darkness we arrived at Jerusalem, tired yet exhilarated. We stopped at a hotel called the "Alhambra," a place with lots of atmosphere. It would be impossible to describe the effect and experience of Jerusalem, a city that had known Christ. You could spend a lifetime there learning new things about the Biblical history around you. We crammed as much as we could in the two days allotted us in our tight schedule, visiting the Dome of the Rock, the Wailing Wall, the Church of the Holy Sepulcher, the Church of the Nativity, and the Garden of Gethsemane. We climbed the steps leading to Calvary, which was the path Christ took bearing his heavy burden, the cross. Here, I wish no shrine had been built—just three wooden crosses would have told the story far more poignantly. Jesus was a man of great simplicity.

The most beautiful and meaningful spot we visited was the Garden of Gethsemane. The olive trees in the garden were old and gnarled. They looked as if they might easily have been growing at the time Christ was there to pray. It was the most restful and peaceful place I have ever visited.

That afternoon our party drove to Bethlehem. We visited the Church of the Nativity. Each of us knelt down and touched the spot where Jesus was supposed to have been born. It was only a few weeks until Christmas and pilgrims had begun to arrive from the far corners of the world.

On our return trip to Jerusalem we saw camel trains silhouetted against the sky, and shepherds tending their sheep, just as they did in Christ's time. The night was cold and crisp and the sky a soft velvety black. One lone star shone in the heavens. If you closed your eyes a moment, it would have been easy to recreate the birth of Christ in your own heart.

Turkey and Greece

The next morning we flew back to Beirut, changed planes and flew to Istanbul, Turkey. The *Escambia* had already departed with the General and Mary on board. We were all to meet in Greece.

Upon our arrival in Turkey, the Embassy sent a car and a member of the staff to meet us and take us back to the Embassy for the night. We spent the next day sightseeing. First we visited the St. Sophia, or the Blue Mosque, and the Mosque of Suleiman the Magnificent. Then we took in the bazaar. At lunchtime we returned to the Embassy where we dined on the terrace, overlooking the Bosphorus. It was a beautiful sight to behold. One of the ships of our Navy was in dock there, so we saw sailors all over the place.

At three o'clock we boarded the plane, bound for Greece.

We had not been in our hotel room in Athens for more than ten minutes when I looked out the window to view our surroundings, and saw what appeared to be a demonstration going on in the street below. "Oh no," Lister said. "That is just a bunch of college boys celebrating after a football game."

"Then why do you think they are carrying signs demanding freedom for Cypress, and the Fire Department is turning the fire hoses on them?" I asked.

In a few minutes the crowd dispersed. There was trouble brewing ahead.

Shortly afterwards our telephone rang and we received an invitation from the Palace to attend a small reception that afternoon for members of Congress who were in Athens on a tour. The American Ambassador, Jack Purefoy, had heard of our arrival and asked that we be included.

We entered the Palace, ascended the red carpeted stairs, and were announced to their Royal Highness, King Paul and Queen Frederica. King Paul was a tall, handsome blond. He was the cousin of Prince Philip, consort of Queen Elizabeth of the British Commonwealth.

After the guests had all been introduced, Queen Frederica turned to Lister and said, "Senator, the last Alabamian I had the pleasure to meet was an admiral who was here during the war. He called me *Honey Child*."

Whereupon one of the Congressmen joined into the conversation, "Senator, if Mrs. Hill had not been here, would you have addressed Her Royal Highness as Honey Child?"

Lister paused a moment before answering, "But," he said, "Mrs. Hill *is* here."

Everybody laughed heartily, breaking the ice.

Having been well fed at the Palace, we decided to take a stroll around the city, ending at a sidewalk café. We sat and drank coffee and ate pistachio nuts purchased from vendors. Athens is beautiful at this season. The parks were particularly festive as the double rows of orange trees were laden with fruit.

The next day, Ambassador Purefoy invited the visiting Congressmen and us for Thanksgiving dinner at his home. The Purefoys were gracious hosts. It had been a fun party. (A few months after our visit we heard that the Ambassador had been killed in an automobile accident. He had been an extremely popular man, who had performed his duties well.)

That evening the *Escambia* docked in the harbor, which was a short distance from Athens. We were delighted to see Mary and L.L. again after our separation in Beirut. The next day we all climbed the hill to reach the Acropolis. Along the roadside we passed "Mars Hill," where St. Paul addressed the Athenians. "In Him we live and move and have our being."

As we approached the Parthenon, we paused to view the immortal beauty of this great temple. The south side of the Acropolis has two theatres built into the hillside. On the east you see the theatre of Dionysus, where many of the Greek tragedies and comedies have been staged. On the west stand the ruins of Odeon, a concert hall built about A.D. 161 by Herod Atticus.

Before departing we sat upon a small wall to see the magnificent view of Athens.

ROME

Dusk found us boarding the *Escambia* and sailing away into the sunset. We had experienced a day of fascinating history, and superb beauty. Many of the passengers who had sailed with us from New York had reached their destination and departed. The few who were still with us expected to return to New York or Boston.

On reaching Naples next day, we left the ship for a trip to Rome and Florence. The black marble station in Rome is the handsomest I have ever seen. It was the pride of Mussolini. We stopped at the Hotel Excelsior. The Eternal City captured me from the beginning. Rome has so many fountains, sculptures, paintings by Old Masters, historic churches, and cathedrals. Most of all I loved the warm-hearted Italians.

Our first day in Rome we lunched at "Alfredoes," and were shown the gold spoon and fork which Mary Pickford and Douglas Fairbanks had given him. Alfredo danced about as he served us with the gold spoon and fork, making a ceremony of it.

Our guide asked us if we would like to have our picture taken with Alfredo to hang on the wall of the restaurant alongside the pictures of the many celebrities who had dined at this famous place. I don't know whether the photograph of the four Hills is still hanging on the wall or not. It was probably taken down a few days after our departure. But I am glad I still have a copy to remind me of the good time we had. Lister stays so busy and works so hard, we have taken very few vacations.

Across the street from Alfredoes is a famous fountain, Trevi. I could not resist tossing in a coin, with the wish that we would some day return to Rome.

On our last day we visited the Vatican and St. Peters. We saw the Pieta and Moses, the magnificent sculptures of Michelangelo. Each of these art treasures is worth a trip to Rome. After going through many of the rooms in the Cathedral, we came to the Sistine Chapel. This is my favorite chapel in the Vatican. Before leaving I purchased a miniature of the Sistine Madonna, intending it for a gift to a friend. When time came to part with it, I found that I could not. The friend received a different gift.

We spent two wonderful days and nights in Rome, and the third day we took the train to Perugia. To our surprise we found that there was no diner on the train. Either you provided your own lunch or purchased it from one of the many vendors in each station. L.L. attracted the attention of a vendor and bought a long loaf of French bread, a package of cheese, and a bottle of wine to wash it down.

By prearrangement, a car and chauffeur awaited us at the station in Perugia. On our way to Florence we passed through many charming villages, including Assisi. We particularly wanted to visit the Basilica in Assisi, and to pay our respects to one of the most beloved Saints in the world. St. Francis' bones are interred in the Basilica. I keep his prayer near at all times. Many of my friends have a St. Francis bird feeding station.

FLORENCE

Florence was our destination. Towards dark, bicycles began coming at us from every direction. This was the rush hour. I don't know how our driver managed to prevent a collision.

While we were in Florence we stayed at the Hotel Excelsior. Following lunch, we visited the Plazzo Pitti. Here we saw many art treasures by Old Masters. Raphael's *Madonna of the Chair* is perhaps the best known of the paintings in this gallery.

Before returning to the Hotel Excelsior, we went shopping on the Ponte Vecchio. During World War II several of the bridges that crossed the Arno River were destroyed, but the Ponte Vecchio was spared. It holds a special place in the hearts of the Florentines.

I was a bit extravagant in Florence, purchasing a gold leaf mirror and a tablecloth for myself.

It was no wonder that Elizabeth and Robert Browning chose to live in Florence. There was much to do and to see. We were shown the house the Brownings occupied while they were living there.

END OF JOURNEY

Regretfully, after two wonderful days in Florence, we took a train for Genoa, Italy. Here, we boarded our ship. There would be no more ports until we reached the States. The day before we landed was my birthday. Lister planned a surprise birthday celebration for me, inviting our group of the friends from the cruise. Each person brought a small remembrance: scarves, perfumes, and cards. Mary Hill gave me a coin necklace she had purchased in Damascus. She then handed me a card from my mother, and a painting that I had admired on the trip. Mama had sent Mary a check to make the purchase. It was a very happy occasion for me. We did hate to say goodbye to the group and for the cruise to end.

The next morning we docked in Boston Harbor, caught a train for Washington, and were home in time for supper. As soon as I could, I telephoned Henrietta in Alabama, to let her know we were back home. The first piece of news she told me was that my mother had been seriously ill while I was away but would let no one write me about her illness. This came as a shock in spite of the fact that Mama was out of the hospital.

The second piece of news was also a shock. Josephine Black had died and had been buried the morning of the day of our return. Josephine was truly a lovely person and I will never cease to miss her.

The 1952 Chicago DNC

Adlai Stevenson had already won the nomination for the Presidency on the Democratic ticket, but the Convention had yet to choose a candidate for VP. With Stevenson's endorsement of John Sparkman, that practically sealed the deal.

I was talking to a group of Alabamians when I saw Dick Harkness, the well-known news commentator for NBC. Dick motioned me away from the crowd. "Who do you hear mentioned for VP?" he asked.

"I don't hear anyone mentioned except John Sparkman," I answered.

Lister and I returned to the hotel quite late. We were dead tired and hoped to get a little sleep. Our lights were turned out about two o'clock. We couldn't have been asleep long when the telephone rang. It was John Sparkman. "Henrietta, could I speak to Lister?"

Lister was now awake. He took the receiver and listened a moment. "I will be glad to place your name in nomination. What time to you want me to be at Convention Hall?" Lister hung up the phone, and he turned to me. "I have to be at the Convention at nine o'clock in the morning, and I have to write my speech beforehand. Wake me up at six." With that, he turned over and went back to sleep. It was the magic hour of four A.M.; things always seem to gel at that hour at a convention.

Knowing that I would never awaken in time, I got out of bed and went into the bathroom and took a bath to help me stay awake. Then I sat in a chair and read a magazine until six. I shook Lister. "Time to get up." As he crawled out of bed, I crawled back in. When I awoke again, Lister had left. Wives at a political convention have to learn to fend for themselves and to act as secretaries for their husbands. Any phone call might be important. But it is a lot more fun if you know what is going on, and participate.

Lister's nominating speech for John Sparkman was a beautiful tribute. When the demonstrations began, Allison Raines (wife of Congressman Albert Raines of Alabama) picked up a large placard for Sparkman. I took up the other side and together we marched in the parade for Sparkman, and the glory of Alabama.

The Hand

In 1948 Estes Kefauver, the Senator from Tennessee, ran on the Democratic ticket in the primary for the nomination to the Senate. Ed Crump, the political boss of Memphis, opposed Kefauver, supporting Tom Stewart.

During the campaign, Boss Crump made the remark that Estes had no more sense than a coon. This remark backfired. Estes purchased a coonskin cap and wore it all during the campaign. Kids all over the country adopted the fad; this was worth a million dollars in free advertisement for Kefauver, who won easily his seat in the Senate.

A month before the 1952 Democratic Convention took place in Chicago, Estes came calling on Lister. The two of them sat on our porch chatting. I was dying to eavesdrop but had to wait until our caller left to ask, "What was all that about?"

"Estes is one of the most disarming persons I have ever met," said Lister. "He asked me to be his Secretary of National Defense should he receive the Democratic nomination for the Presidency. Then he added that it did not matter whether I supported him or not, he still wanted me because he felt that I was the best qualified man he knew for that position."

By this time, Lister had served fourteen years on the House Military Affairs Committee, and was Chairman of the Committee for a year and a half before moving on to the Senate, where he served on the Senate Military Affairs Committee, and as assistant leader or Whip.

Estes lost out in the Democratic Convention to John Sparkman.

Just prior to the 1956 Democratic Convention, we entertained some of our neighbors at a small dinner in our home. A few hours before the guests arrived I was scanning Bill White's new book *The Citadel* when my eyes fell upon a comment not at all complimentary to Estes: "The Crime Investigating Committee was a road show for Estes, and that the Senator was not in the inner circle of the Southerners in the Senate." It was too late to do anything about it, except hope for the best.

The Kefauvers were a little late in arriving. Nancy looked lovely as always. After shaking hands all around, Estes took me aside and asked, "Henrietta, will you please take me to the telephone; I have to make a call." I obliged by leading him to the library. "The telephone book is in the drawer of the table," I said as I started to leave the room.

"Don't go—I want to ask you about your guests. Who is the lady in the red dress?" Before we left the library, Estes had received rundown on all the guests present.

We had barely been seated in the dining room when I saw Estes lean forward to speak to Bill White. *Oh my!* I thought, *Here it comes.* "Bill," said Estes in his soft southern accent, "why did you write the things you did about me in your last book, *The Citadel*? I could have straightened you out." I don't remember Bill's reply, but before the evening was over they were chatting away gaily with all their differences apparently resolved.

In an effort to change the conversation, I asked, "Estes, where did you meet your wife Nancy?" This seemed to do the trick.

In the summer of 1956, Estes decided to try again to obtain the Democratic nomination for Presidency. He was again disappointed. Adlai Stevenson, chosen once again as the Democratic nominee for the Presidency, declared the race for the Vice Presidency nomination would be wide open. Normally the race for the VP is cut and dried and uninteresting. Any candidate who has enough votes to win the nomination for the Presidency can name his own running mate. Stevenson chose to break this tradition.

Lister and I watched the convention on TV. It was truly exciting. Right in the middle of the voting I had to leave for an appointment at the beauty parlor. I could hardly bear to miss a minute of it. Kefauver and Jack Kennedy were running neck to neck in a real horse race. As I walked into the beauty parlor the lady at the appointment desk asked, "Are you Mrs. Hill? There is a telephone call for you." It was Lister, calling to let me know Estes won. It was a tight race until the end.

It was a cold, brisk day in December 1962. Isabel Griffin, Catherine Jordan, and I were the guests of Betty Hogate for luncheon that noon. The log fire and warm sunshine streaming through the picture windows at the Chevy Chase Winter Sports Center made us forget the coldness outside. After luncheon we each took our coffee cups and sat by the window to watch the skaters glide by on the ice rink below. Ice skating has always enchanted me, but there was no place to learn the sport in Alabama: it rarely even snows.

Most of the children we watched skate by had learned in early childhood. Some of the older people we saw had mastered the art years ago and were experts. One gentleman we saw was clearly not in this latter group. I soon recognized it was Estes. Two lovely girls were supporting him, one on each side. Even then he could hardly manage to stay on his feet. Once he ventured out alone; at least he was game. His wife Nancy, born and raised in Scotland, glided gracefully by. This was clearly not Estes' sport. The Kefauvers made a charming family group at play.

A few months later I saw Senator Kefauver in the Senate dining room. He was making the rounds, visiting with each group and shaking their hands. Lister called the tall slender Tennessean to come over to our table and shake hands with our guests, Vincent Townsend, publisher of the *Birmingham News*, and his wife Julia, and Ann and Jim Free, correspondents for the *News*. Senator Kefauver had long, thin hands; his handshake was warm and firm. Because his hand was forever extended to someone, the *Capitol Pages* nicknamed him "The Hand."

In August 1963, Estes died suddenly of a ruptured aorta at the Naval Hospital in Bethesda, Maryland. He was only sixty years old.

Nancy and the children were away on a vacation out West. Surviving him were his wife Nancy, his three daughters (Eleanor, Diane, and Gale), and son David.

The other day we received an invitation to attend a party given by the Kefauver Memorial Committee, who hope to raise enough money to erect a suitable memorial to the Tennessee Senator.

You wonder sometimes how to assess a man like Kefauver. A man who in childhood knew what he wanted and went after it. He was an indefatigable worker, a man of integrity, and a lone wolf. When he came to Washington as a member of the House of Representatives he was like a fresh mountain breeze, and he came pretty close to realizing his lifelong ambition to become President.

CHRISTMAS, 1957

Lister, Jr. and Catherine Gore were married on August 25, 1957 in St. Margaret's Chapel in the Washington Cathedral.

The first day of the wedding the Senate was in the midst of a filibuster. Lister, Sr. was supposed to serve as his son's best man. Senator Strom Thurmond of South Carolina held the floor. During a Quorum Call, Lister sought out the South Carolina Senator. "Strom, how long are you going to talk? My son is being married this afternoon and I am supposed to be best man in the wedding."

"Stay as long as you want to," said Strom. "I will keep on talking until you get back."

He did!

After a short honeymoon, the newlyweds moved into a small apartment in Cambridge, Massachusetts. Lister, Jr. matriculated at the Harvard Law School. Three years later, we had a full-fledged barrister in the family. Their first child—a son, William Preston—waited to put in his appearance until his mama and daddy were settled in Montgomery, Alabama.

National Institutes of Health

On June 30, 1960, Lister and I drove out to the National Institutes of Health in Bethesda, Maryland, to attend the dedication of the new Division of Biologies Standards Building. King Bhumibol Adulyadej of Thailand was the principal speaker; he stressed the importance of international cooperation in the fight against disease and paid tribute to the humanitarian objectives of the National Institutes of Health. "It is fortunate," he said, "that medical science recognizes no national boundaries."

Referring to the role of the NIH, he continued, "The Institutes are in fact waging a war—a hot war and not a cold war—a war against disease, waged for the benefit of all mankind." He termed the new building another powerful arm for use in that noble struggle, and congratulated the Institutes upon their acquisition of this additional modern weapon.

King Bhumibol, in this country with Queen Sirikit for a brief state visit, was asked to participate in the dedication ceremonies because of his role in promoting health measures in his own country and his interest in the SEATO-NIH Cholera Research Project. He spoke before an audience of one thousand invited guests, including Congressional and Government leaders and Thai officials.

NIH Director Dr. James Shannon delivered a brief address of welcome, and Public Health Surgeon General Burney introduced the guest and speakers.

Lister emphasized the role of medical research: "Today, medicine and medical research offer the one great opportunity for cooperation and understanding among nations of the world. Medicine speaks a universal language—it speaks to all peoples and all lands, and a victory in medicine by any nation is a victory shared by all mankind. I am convinced, that medicine, with its resources and influences fully mobilized, can do more for permanent peace than all the billions of dollars being poured into the armaments race."

Representative Fogarty of Rhode Island, who is Chairman of the House Subcommittee on Appropriations, recalled Dr. Shannon's first appearance as NIH Director before that committee four years ago: "At that time, Dr. Shannon brought to the attention of the Committee the accomplishments and expanding responsibilities of the newly formed Division of Biologies Standards.

(Published in "On the Record," July 19, 1960)

JUNE 30, 1960

When the ceremonies concluded, Lister and I attended a luncheon honoring their Majesties, the King and Queen of Thailand. Queen Sirikit wore exquisite clothes (especially designed for her) to every public appearance in Washington. Both their Majesties spoke flawless English. Lister had the honor of sitting next to the Queen. He reported her to be a delightful conversationalist, as was King Bhumibol Adulyadej.

I was seated between Dr. Shannon and one of the Thailand officials. During the luncheon I learned a lot of fascinating history about Thailand. Prince Mahee of Songkhla, the father of the King, studied medicine at the Harvard Medical School. It was during his residency that his son was born in December of 1927. (Prince Mahee was at that time not in succession for the Kingship; because of the sudden death of his brother, he succeeded to the throne in June 1946 as King Rama IX.) King Mongkut, the great-grandfather of King Bhumibol, was the monarch on whose life the novel *Anna and the King of Siam* was based. When the play *The King and I* was produced on Broadway, the name of the novel had been changed.

Later, the official party visited Harvard and attended the unveiling of a plaque at Mt. Auburn Hospital in the room in which King Bhumibol was born. He has the distinction of being the only King ever to be born in the United States.

Dr. Shannon asked me if I had ever taken the tour of the research center at NIH. He seemed surprised when I said no. "You really should. Lister is responsible for most of what you see out here. I can set up a tour for you and a few of your friends with a day's notice." I thanked the Doctor and promised to call him very soon. At this moment the Royal guests began saying their goodbyes and left shortly. They were a charming couple. I have not met anyone who traveled in the Far East who did not exclaim over the graciousness of the people of Thailand. As we drove out of the grounds of NIH, I could not help being proud of Lister and all he and done to promote medical research.

It was not a lack of interest but an accident that greatly impaired my walking which delayed my return visit to NIH by two years. One morning, Janet Terry, the wife of the then-Public Health Surgeon General Dr. Luther Terry, called to invite me to lunch at the Institutes and to take the long awaited tour of the research center. Perhaps the children's wing of the Heart Institute was the most appealing to us. Some of the patients were recuperating from open heart surgery; others were waiting their time. A few of them were in wheelchairs, having undergone surgery only a few days before. All showed remarkable courage.

One of our group, Mrs. Donald Hogate, had a twelve year old niece who needed open heart surgery to repair a heart leakage. Mrs. Hogate began asking questions as to the procedure for acceptance of patients. She was told that her niece's present doctor would have to refer her to the Institute, and would have to send Susie's case record to the Heart Center. The staff would then study her record, give her a physical, and determine whether to operate. That was all two years ago. Susie had her open-heart operation at NIH and eleven months later won the junior diving contest and was second in the swimming competition in the annual YWCA swimming meet in Norfolk, VA. Had Susie not submitted to heart surgery, her life expectancy would have been only a few brief years.

Tucked away someplace in the Medical Library at NIH is a documented account of the first successful suture of the human heart. Dr. Luther L. Hill—Lister's father—did this in 1902 in Montgomery, Alabama. A Negro boy named Henry Merrick was stabbed in the heart by another teenager.

The removal of the knife was done on a kitchen table in a Negro cabin by the light from an oil lamp. Harry Merrick lived to grow up, but as fate would have it, while in Chicago he was again stabbed in the heart.

But this operation paved the way for countless open heart surgeries.

SHORTLY AFTER MY VISIT to the Research Center, I was invited to talk to the Senate Ladies Red Cross Unit on the NIH. The Senate Ladies met every Tuesday in the Red Cross rooms in the Old Senate Office building to sew, knit, or roll bandages. In the last few years, the Ladies have planned a speaking program to try to help entertain the workers, as they toiled away.

Here is my contribution:

A friend of my mother's once said to me, "My dear, when you reach my age, your basis for congeniality with your friends is: *Do you have heart trouble, arthritis, or stomach trouble?* Knowing that interest in health is universal, I have chosen as my topic for today medical research at the National Institutes of Health at Bethesda, Maryland, and at other Institutes throughout the United States that received grants in aid from the Government through NIH. I am proud to say that Lister had a large part in creating this great medical research center.

There are seven separate Institutes of Health which make up the National Institutes of Health at Bethesda—the Institutes of Arthritis and Metabolic Diseases; Cancer; Heart; Mental Diseases; Allergy and Infectious Diseases; Neurological Diseases and Blindness; and Dental.

The research being done by scientists at NIH and at other Institutes around the country who are sharing grants is too vast to discuss in the limited time which I have here this morning, but it was my thought that you might be interested in a few of the discoveries which are calculated to keep you in good health for the rest of your days, and to prevent you from answering Gabriel's call before your allotted time.

We have only to point to President Eisenhower and Senate Majority Leader Lyndon Johnson to realize the value of Medical Research in heart diseases. A few years ago, cholesterol and anti-coagulants were unheard of. Heart disease, which is still the nation's number one killer, took 900,00 lives last year.

Dr. Michael DeBakey and his group, who have received grants in aid from NIH have proved that forty percent of all strokes arise from artery blockage in the neck and chest and not from the brain, and can be treated surgically, preventing paralysis by removing the impaired artery and replacing it with a plastic tube. (This same Dr. Mike DeBakey operated on the Duke of Windsor in Houston in 1956, removing an aneurysm.)

Patients suffering from mental illnesses have long occupied over half of all our hospital beds. The development of the tranquilizers through medical research has resulted in the first reduction in the mental hospital population.

A few years ago, medical science was only able to save one out of four persons stricken with cancer. Today, one out of every three recovers. In the U.S. there is still an average of 250,000 deaths from this dread disease. The National Cancer Institute spent $58 million on cancer research in 1958. This monstrous disease cost our economy $12 billion annually in productive loss.

Leukemia, which is cancer of the blood, is second only to lung cancer in its rising incidence. Scientists doing research on leukemia think they have been able to isolate a virus in leukemia patients that causes the disease. If this theory proves to be true after sufficient tests have been made, it will be only a short while until a serum can be developed such as the Salk vaccine for the prevention of polio.

As a result of the work financed by the NIH of a group of scientists at the University of Tennessee, cancer of the vagina is easily detected in an early stage by a simple smear test, which makes possible the surgical removal of the cancer.

Until a short time ago, a patient suspected of having a brain cancer had to undergo a test, for diagnostic purposes, which caused excruciating pain, and which often proved ineffectual. This test is no longer necessary, because of the development of a machine at NIH that charts the brain waves electronically.

Tuberculosis, which was once the number one killer, has dropped eighty percent in the past fifteen years. Streptomycin, the drug that has made this possible, was discovered in 1944. When it was first put on the market, it cost $250 a gram. Because the NIH stepped in to synthesize this drug, the price dropped to ten dollars a gram, thus making it available to thousands who could not afford it in the beginning.

Think what it means to a diabetic to be able to swallow a pill instead of having to take medication hypodermically several times a day for years on end.

I could go on and on, but I cannot leave this subject without telling that NIH has developed an adhesive that can glue bones together and has been used on dogs to repair teeth that grow new tissues and are just as good as new. I for one hope it means that I will never have to own a set of false teeth.

We are prone to forget the wonderful medical contributions that have been given to us by other nations. Microbiology came from Holland, Immunology with Vaccination came from Great Britain, Bacteriology came from Pasteur in France, antisepsis and asepsis which made modern surgery possible came from Joseph Lister in England, Sulfonamides from Germany, Penicillin from Great Britain, Insulin from Canada, Cortisone and Anesthesia from the U.S., and Rauwolfia (which is so helpful in the treatment of high blood pressure and mental illness) from India. Last year Lister introduced a bill in Congress known as the International Health and Medical Research Act of 1959. This act would create an Institute in connection with NIH for the exchange of medical knowledge and research with countries throughout the world. As Dr. Howard Rusk of New York said, "Medicine has never been anything but international. You go back in history and it is the most beautiful evidence of Internationalism that exists in the world."

Can you think of a better way to let the world know that we are concerned in saving life instead of destroying it?

Ike & Mamie

Ike and Mamie were warm friends of ours even before he became President. We were never among their most intimate friends, but President and Mrs. Eisenhower were more than gracious. Each year when they gave a dinner honoring the Speaker of the House, Mr. Sam Rayburn of Texas, Lister and I were included. On one occasion Lawrence Welk came to entertain.

IT WAS THE NSID (National Society of Interior Decorators) that contributed the first unsolicited gift toward a restoration project for the White House. Up to that time apparently no one had thought of such a thing. During the Eisenhower Administration the Society gave the lovely period furniture which graces the Diplomatic Reception Room. Later, while Mrs. Kennedy was completing the White House restoration, the NSID at her request added the authentic wallpaper, hand-blocked by Martin Zuber, circa 1830. This paper was designed to commemorate Lafayette's visit and it extends the full circumference of the oval walls.

Peter Hill, a collector and connoisseur of rare antiques, discovered the Zuber wallpaper and rescued it from a house in Maryland that was being demolished. Mr. Hill paid the wreckers fifty dollars for the wallpaper. He removed it from the walls of the house with a putty knife, without damage. The NSID bought it for twelve thousand dollars.

There are many other choice replacements to admire throughout the "President's House," but the Diplomatic Room is by far my favorite.

IT IS CUSTOMARY FOR the First Lady to entertain the Senate Ladies Red Cross Unit every spring. The Senate Ladies return the courtesy, entertaining the First Lady and the Wives of the President's Cabinet at a luncheon at the Senate Office Building. Former Members come from far and wide to attend these luncheons.

Mrs. Eisenhower gave one of the gayest parties. The main entrance was elaborately decorated with dogwood trees and vines. In the dining room, Easter rabbits, birds, and flowers banked the mantel. Each place at the table was marked by a miniature hatbox—which contained a miniature Easter bonnet made by "Sally Victor." After a short period Mrs. Eisenhower tired of the song of the mechanical birds and called to a butler: "Turn off the birds."

PART FIVE

1960–1965

The 1962 Inauguration Blizzard

O ur daughter Henrietta, her husband Charles Hubbard, and their two sons Clark and Lister arrived in Washington to witness the Inauguration of John F. Kennedy, 35th President of the United States.

The Hubbards lived in Montgomery, and neither of the boys had ever seen a snowstorm. For weeks before their arrival, the older son, Clark, prayed for it to snow while they were in Washington. The night before the Kennedy inauguration it snowed and snowed and snowed, then it sleeted and snowed. The grandchildren were ecstatic.

The next morning at breakfast we were all exchanging experiences of the night before when Charles walked in. He said to Clark, "Son, if you can get all your prayers answered as well as this one, we ought to make a preacher out of you. In the meantime, please ask the Lord to turn off the snow. We have about enough of it." [Clark is now an Episcopal priest.]

On the eve of the inauguration, many parties were planned for the visiting dignitaries. It had just begun to snow as Henrietta, Charles, and I set out for the Sheraton Park Hotel to attend the Governors' Reception. It had been our intention to welcome Alabama's Governor John Patterson. Then we thought we might look for some of the movie stars and other celebrities. Most of them were already gone. Our next destination was a buffet supper at the Phil Graham's home in Georgetown. Philip Graham is the publisher of the *Washington Post*. Lister was to meet us there. It was rumored that the Kennedys were expected to attend.

We were ready to move on to the Graham's but a blizzard was now raging outside. The taxi situation at the Sheraton remained the same— no taxies were available. Around nine o'clock, exhausted and hungry, I telephoned Senator and Mrs. Spessard Holland of Florida, who have an apartment at the Sheraton Park. Thank goodness she was home. "Mary," I said, "could we come up to your apartment to rest a while? We have been here in the lobby for hours and there is no place to sit."

The Hollands gave us a very warm welcome. Mary went even further—she fed us. I can testify that Senator Holland has the best cook in town. Mary scrambled eggs for us and fed us the last bit of bacon plus Florida grapefruit, and lots of hot coffee.

Not wanting to keep the Hollands up any longer, we went back to the lobby of the hotel, hoping for better luck in finding a taxi. Fortunately for us, Charles spotted an Alabama patrolman who had come to Washington as a part of the Governor's entourage. His car had a high-powered engine and was equipped with snow tires. Better still, he offered to take us home. As we were about to pull away from the hotel, Mrs. Stephen Young of Ohio ran out calling to me, "Mrs. Hill, Mrs. Hill, please take me home with you." We did. Her house is not very far from ours. We had been away from home over six hours. It was wonderful to be home and to be warm again.

Lister had his adventure too. He left the Capitol at four o'clock hoping to get away from the traffic. Apparently everybody else had the same idea. It was bumper to bumper from start to finish. Cars were stalled or stuck all along the streets.

Lister was driving a brand new Oldsmobile, which had been delivered to him early that morning. He was amazed when the battery gave up the struggle near Dupont Circle. Lister abandoned it and set out on foot for the Mayflower Hotel three blocks away, where he hoped to find a taxi.

The Mayflower Hotel lobby was crowded with stranded people who seemed to have settled down for the night. After a bit of thawing, Lister renewed his efforts to find transportation to Spring Valley. There was one taxi pulling out when Lister spied him. The driver at first refused, but a ten-dollar bill changed his mind.

Only grandchildren could have persuaded me to brave that Arctic cold to witness the ceremonies in which the President and the Vice President take the oath of office. We never could get to our seats for the ceremonies. We took the only available ones we saw.

Jackie looked adorable. The Kennedys make a handsome couple. The words of Jack Kennedy will long live in the minds of all who heard them spoken, "Ask not what your country can do for you—ask what you can do for your country."

To view the parade, Lister had arranged for us to sit on one of the balconies of the Old Senate Office Building. We lunched beforehand in the restaurant in the building, then took our places on the balcony. If any of us became too chilled we could go back into the building to thaw out. Our visitors left the next day. We were sorry to have our young people leave us; we see them so seldom. As the taxi driver deposited the four Hubbards at the railway station, he added, "Have a nice trip."

Clark spoke up: "We have had our trip."

The driver repeated, "Have a nice trip."

Clark looked puzzled. "I told you we have already had our trip."

AMERICANS WILL ALWAYS REMEMBER Jacqueline Kennedy for the superb job she did in refurbishing the White House. Like Dolly Madison, Jackie brought glamour to the President's house.

When I read in the paper of Mrs. Kennedy's new project, I could not resist writing her a little note saying, "Bravo! Congratulations on your plans to renovate the White House. I do hope you will have the brown marble mantels in the East Room replaced by the Italian white marble mantels which were removed when the White House was rebuilt."

The mantels have not been replaced, but last spring when I attended a luncheon at the White House I noticed the brown marble mantels had been painted white. The White House is now furnished with a rare collection of famous paintings, some on loan and some donated for a permanent collection. In each of the rooms are priceless antiques of the period of the rooms in which they are placed.

When you see the daily lineup, four abreast on the sidewalk around the grounds, waiting for the White House tour, we are grateful to Mrs. Kennedy for stimulating the American public's interest in a heritage they can be proud of.

Honoring Ladybird

MAY 4, 1961
75TH CLUB HONORING MRS. LYNDON JOHNSON [SPEECH GIVEN
  BY HENRIETTA HILL]

The election of the 75th Congress brought to Washington one of the largest Democratic majorities ever to be elected. This Congress became known as the Roosevelt, or New Deal Congress. I recall that columnist Ray Clapper exclaimed, "The Republicans just held out Maine and Vermont—for breeding purposes."

Shortly after Congress convened, Mrs. Albert Carter organized the wives of the members of the 75th Congress into a club with Mrs. John Murdock as first President. Our membership consisted of about one hundred twenty five members with the ratio of three-to-one Democratic. Today our group has shrunk to sixteen members in the Washington area, with only nine of those still in Congress. During the past twenty-four years the surviving members have grown increasingly fond of each other and party affiliations are all but forgotten.

We are proud of our club. Among our members we have an historian, Mrs. Murdock; a Senator, Margaret Chase Smith; a Vice Presidential Nominee's wife, Ivo Sparkman—and I am even going to brag on my own family: the co-author of the Hill-Burton Hospital Act, which has built 5,500 hospitals and clinics throughout the U.S. (By 1966 the number of hospitals built under the Hill-Burton Hospital Construction Act numbered over eight thousand nursing homes, hospitals, and clinics in the United States.) I won't tell you of all our virtues, for this occasion was planned as an appreciation day for one of our beloved members—Lady Bird Johnson, the wife of our Vice President.

During the campaign last fall, I had the pleasure of riding across the State of Alabama on the LBJ Campaign Special. Lady Bird was a bit nervous, for in a sense she was on home territory. "What shall I say she asked me?"

"Just be your own sweet self," I replied.

And that is exactly what she did. Her speech began like this: "My mother and father both came from Alabama, and I have had many happy times as a child visiting relatives in Autuga County, eating watermelon, and going swimming in Mulberry Creek."

About this time, two or three dozen of Lady Bird's Alabama relatives began piling on the back of the train, which made it difficult to hear Lyndon's speech—but he need not have said a single word—Lady Bird had already captured the crowd.

I have watched Lady Bird preside at the Senate Ladies Red Cross meeting each Tuesday, which she does regularly if she is not flying off to Texas, Africa, or Timbuktu. Wherever she goes or wherever she presides, she does so with charm, with grace, and with dignity. We feel she could hold her own in any position, but we are not honoring her today as the wife of the Vice President, we are paying this tribute to her as a true and loyal friend, and as a member of the 75th Club of whom we are justly proud. We hope that this small token will convey to her our affection and that it will remind her of the many happy times we have had together.

(The gift was a gold charm for a bracelet with *L.B.J.* inscribed, and the date: *May 4, 1961 – 75th Club.*)

Modern Campaigning

March 20, 1962

Today the District Red Cross presented me with a certificate for thirty years of service in that organization.

Campaign—November 1962

In 1962, Congress did not adjourn until October, which left only three weeks for members to campaign for reelection. There wasn't time for Lister to open a campaign headquarters. His regular office in the Federal Building continued business as usual for the constituents, but the Campaign Headquarters was moved to our home in Montgomery. There were people coming in and out of our house day and night. The telephone rang continuously. I never knew how many people to expect for lunch or dinner. That was Charlie Harvey's (our cook and driver) department.

Without the use of a plane, we could not have covered the territory we did, jumping from the Tennessee Valley to Mobile Bay. We did the short trips by car.

Election Night, November 1962

On the night of the election, Lister's administrative assistant Don Cronin and his wife Mary and our children all came for dinner with us. One of the neighbors sent over a box of delicious cakes, thinking, "This would probably be a long night."

Around seven o'clock Jim Martin (Lister's opponent) was leading. At nine, things looked even worse. Shortly after ten, Lister began to pull up. A number of our friends came to call and to wish us success. The two candidates were neck and neck. Don Cronin and Lister, Jr. took the telephone calls and did the tabulating.

I was in the kitchen for more cake and coffee to serve our callers, the reporters, and photographers. My daughter, Henrietta, threw her arms around my neck and began to cry. "Oh, Mother, I don't want Daddy hurt, he has done so much for so many people, and has worked so hard. I can't bear it." I felt just as upset as my daughter, but I said, "Henrietta, you must cut this out. You must not let the reporters see you crying. Just take a look at your Daddy; he has been magnificent. If he can take it, we can."

A short time later the picture changed. Lister was nudging ahead. It seemed a bit premature to me when the photographers began taking pictures of Lister as the winner. I was surprised—but proud.

FEBRUARY 1963

About eight years ago, Katie Louchheim (Mrs. Walter Louchheim) our Democratic National Committee Woman, conceived the idea that Congressional wives might be helpful in a campaign. Carrie Davis, Lynda Boggs, and a few of the other women who were willing to give several hours a day at National Headquarters were asked to come down to lend a hand. The Committee was swamped with mail, and had very few regular workers. The experiment worked so well that Katie called her Congressional helpers "My Gold."

It was then decided that the Democratic Congressional wives should form an organization known as the "Forum." The purpose of the "Forum" was to swap ideas, and to teach campaign techniques. We were to conduct debates, and study the important bills in Congress. I believe that Pauline Gore of Tennessee was chosen as first President, Grace Kerr as second president, Ivo Sparkman of Alabama third, and I was the fourth President.

At our first meeting of the Forum after the election in 1962, I was asked to tell the other members of the Forum what happened in Alabama in Lister's campaign. My talk was as follows:

In 1962, for the first time in nearly a hundred years, the Republican Party in Alabama made a serious attempt to elect three Representatives and a U.S. Senator to the Congress. The photo finish of the Senate race was watched with interest around the country, with many of the viewers wondering what had happened in Alabama.

Months before the election, Senator Barry Goldwater came to our State to stir up the Conservatives, who in turn seized upon the race issue to inflame the masses of the people. With the Oxford, Mississippi affair next door to us, membership in the KKK, the White Citizens Council, and the John Birch Society grew by leaps and bounds.

Congress stayed in session until three weeks before Election Day. Try explaining to your constituents why you can't come home to campaign. Your enemies are accusing you of overconfidence. If you haven't had a tough campaign in a long time, *Beware!* Your supporters are likely to have grown bored with no activity and will take your re-election for granted. In the last Alabama election, forty percent of the registered voters failed to go to the polls. Democrats in the South have become used to a fight in the Spring Primary, but the General Elections have gone to the Democrats by default. From now on things will be different in the South; the Republicans are well organized and well financed. It has been estimated that they spent $600,000 in the recent race for the U.S. Senate in Alabama. The Republican Party has set out to include the "Solid South." In my opinion, the other Southern states can look for the same vigorous attack two years from now. The most effective ad used in the Alabama race against us was "Send a message to the Kennedys by Jim Martin that the South can *no longer* be taken for granted. Elect Jim Martin to the U.S. Senate." There has been a tendency by some Democrats from outside the South to write the South off. Can the Democratic Party afford to do this? The South still holds the chairmanship of many of the great committees and, if I recall correctly, there were few sweeping victories for the Democrats throughout the country in 1962—some of them were pretty close.

To get back to our race—with only three weeks to campaign, time being of the essence, we decided that TV was our best medium for reaching the most people in the State. Since so few local, small stations have the proper equipment, we hired professionals to produce and record on tape two TV shows. In this way you can cut the bad shots. If you haven't already done so, hire a professional to teach you how to apply makeup for TV. To quote a CBS technician, "TV can be monstrous. It can make or break you." Incidentally, our opponent was young and photogenic. He chose to fight a completely negative campaign. He wasn't for anything, just against everything. He followed closely the Goldwater tactics. "The Democrats are anti-business, the Democrats are socialists, etc."

Lister chose to run a positive campaign, mostly on his record of the past forty years. As far as I remember, he never mentioned his opponent by name. The first of his two TV shows was a half hour question-and-answer period, with four prominent Alabamians asking Lister to discuss his position on the issues of the campaign. In the second show we used a professional to act as narrator for a trip around Alabama to view the Hill-Burton hospitals, health centers, armed forces bases, REA and rural telephone installations, TVA and rivers and harbor developments, and many more things which Lister sponsored or co-authored, including the NIH, the National Medical Library here in Washington, and Book Mobiles throughout every state.

Now as for the women's angle, the Democratic women manned a booth at the State Fair in Montgomery from which they dispensed political brochures and hot coffee to the tired visitors.

The last week of the campaign, our women workers pinned streamers across their bosoms saying, "Vote Nov. 6." On their white hats were other banners saying "Vote Democratic" or "Vote for Lister Hill." They passed out literature from decorated baskets and talked to as many people as they could. We found during the 1960 Kennedy campaign that few people bother to go to a political headquarters, so we sought them out on the streets and in the shopping centers.

Let a worker send out a dozen letters in your behalf and he is far more interested in your campaign. Our older women got a great kick out of being included in addressing envelopes. All this is probably old hat to most of you, but it was a new experience to me, since Lister never had but one other serious race since our marriage. Anyway, here we are back again and a bit wiser. I consider it Lister's greatest victory. The final count gave Lister seven thousand votes ahead of Martin.

In the 1964 Congressional elections my predictions came true—Alabama elected five Republican Congressmen to the House of Representatives.

A Man's Home Is His Castle

SUMMER, 1963

It was late, around eleven-thirty at night. The lights were out and we were fast asleep. Then the telephone rang and a man's voice announced, "I am a reporter from the *Washington Post*. We have been tipped off that your house is being picketed, what about it?"

A bit startled, I exclaimed, "Everything seems to be quite peaceful. We haven't seen any pickets." As soon as I hung up the receiver, I jumped out of bed to look out the window, in time to watch the advance guard arrive by car. Moments later, people from every direction emerged from the darkness. In all, about fifty people congregated in front of our residence.

Each of the participants in the demonstration carried a flashlight and a placard as they tramped back and forth in front of our house. Most of the cards protested, "Police Brutality" and the use of dogs to quell a riot in Birmingham. Our house in Washington sits on the crest of a small hill. A picket ran up to the steps to our front door, rang the doorbell for five minutes, then descended to the sidewalk. A replacement repeated the performance. It was a sort of relay race that continued for an hour or so.

We did not telephone the police, nor did we let the mob in our house. When the police patrol arrived, the Sergeant rapped on our door and called, "Senator, this is the police." We invited him in and gave him a warm welcome. "Senator," continued the officer, "we can run these people in if you want us to. They are violating the District Trespassing Law." We did not wish to press charges against the pickets at that time; since the police stopped them from ringing our doorbell and kept them from crossing our property line, we felt quite secure. The patrol stayed with us the rest of the night, for which we were grateful.

Next morning the pickets were back again. This continued for four or five days. It seemed like a lifetime.

Senator John Sparkman and his wife are neighbors of ours. Fortunately for them, they were out of town. Their pickets joined ours when they discovered the Sparkmans were away.

Four weeks later the pickets were back again. The issue: "Birmingham."

During our siege, I did our marketing very early in the morning before the pickets began their tramp, tramp, tramp back and forth in front of our house. Lister went to his office at the Capital as usual. My days were spent on our back porch. I never let the group see me, but I kept a close watch on their movements.

Several of the young men in the group wore beards. There were as many white demonstrators as colored. One Negro youth kept his nose in a book. I wondered if he was trying to keep up with his homework or was endeavoring to relieve his boredom. A Negro girl tramped all day in bare feet; she wore a knee length red dress that covered her unborn child.

One afternoon a group of teenage boys appeared, each with a large dog on a leash. They began picketing the pickets from the opposite side of the street. This was dynamite. The police quickly disbanded the "Canine Corps."

I was determined, if possible, that no incident should occur. Finally the group disintegrated. One by one they faded away.

I am confident that few, if any, of the marchers were from Alabama. The police had photographs of most of the demonstrators; many had participated in similar activities throughout the city.

During the first days of our being picketed, a former maid of ours, Mamie White, who was home recuperating from an operation, telephoned to inquire about our welfare. "Are those people out there bothering you?"

"No, Mamie, they are not bothering me except to make me very nervous. I am afraid somebody might throw a brick or a stone and set off a riot."

Neither Lister nor I slept soundly during this ordeal.

MAMIE WHITE CAME TO us during the war, in March 1942. I was desperate for help and welcomed her with open arms. Our new maid stayed with us for two weeks without saying anything except "good morning." At the end of our trial period, Mamie came in and formally announced, "I like y'all. I am going to stay." Mamie kept her word; she stayed with us until her death in June 1964. During the war, Lister worked long hours, and Mamie was a great help to me. She loved the children and watched over them when I was out.

In 1964 Mamie had to undergo a second brain tumor operation. We were all very sad but all Mamie would say was, "Well, I guess this is just one of those things."

Assassination

NOVEMBER 22, 1963

"Where were you when President Kennedy was assassinated?" Ask a dozen people, at least nine of them remember. How could anyone forget? I was in Dr. Peterson's office in Bethesda, where I had gone for therapy on my crippled legs (from an accident).

Elizabeth, my therapist, came in with the news. "President Kennedy has been shot. It just came over the radio."

"You must be kidding," I said.

"Why would I joke about a thing like that?" she asked.

"It sounds incredible," I added.

After the death of the President was officially announced, everyone stayed glued to the TV or radio, listening for each word telling of the tragedy. The world was stunned.

The Sunday before the funeral was held, John F. Kennedy lay in state in the East Room of the White House. Lister stayed home with a bad cold, but I went to the Capitol with my neighbors, Senator and Mrs. Clinton Anderson of New Mexico. Arrangements had been made for a fleet of chauffer-driven cars to shuttle back and forth from the Capitol to the White House, transporting all members of the Senate and their wives who wished to pay their respects to their slain President. The House members and wives were afforded the same privilege.

Senator and Mrs. Anderson, Senator Robert Byrd of West Virginia, and I shared a car. As we rode down Pennsylvania Avenue, I kept thinking of the radiant young couple that traveled this same route barely three years prior, the dramatic snowstorm—and the cold drizzling rain of this day.

The front door of the White House was draped in black crepe. Inside the East Room some of the windows were also draped in black. We slowly walked past the flag-covered casket, then out through the Diplomatic Room into a waiting limousine. It was a melancholy day.

The next day the President's casket was moved to the rotunda of the Capitol where it lay in state for all to see.

Because of the lack of space in St. Matthew's Cathedral, only a few Congressional wives were invited to the funeral. In spite of his cold, Lister attended the services. Attached to the back of each seat was the name of the person expected to occupy it. In each seat was laid a pamphlet, on the cover of which was a photograph of John F. Kennedy. Inside the book, the funeral services were translated into English so that most participants could understand the ceremony. [The service was traditionally recited in Latin.]

Some of the notables attending the funeral were Prince Philip of Great Britain, President de Gaulle of France, President Eamon de Valera of Ireland, Queen Frederica of Greece, and Haile Selassie of Ethiopia.

A few short miles away the President was laid to rest in Arlington National Cemetery.

The two moments that were the most dramatic to me on TV were the oath taking of President Johnson on the plane, and the funeral procession of President Kennedy with his widow following behind the caisson. Each showed the tremendous courage of Jacqueline Kennedy—she was magnificent.

Lyndon Johnson was well equipped to take over the Presidency. The fact that the Government continued to function without a hitch greatly impressed the leaders of the world. A South American woman I know expressed admiration at the smoothness with which the Johnson Administration took over the government. "That is the difference between a democracy and a dictatorship," said she. "In our country, there would have been a revolution."

THE JOHNSONS HAVE ENTERTAINED more than any other "First Family" in my thirty-eight years in Washington. Their intention seems to be to share the White House with everybody, and to make every visitor feel at home. It is not unusual for Mrs. Johnson to take guests on a tour of the family living quarters.

The First Lady has demonstrated interest in the thousands of tourists waiting patiently in line (four abreast) to see the interior of the White House. For their comfort, benches and drinking fountains have been added along the way to the entrance gate.

Mrs. Johnson has her own project, "beautification of all parks and highways." This spring Pennsylvania Avenue was a riot of color with flowers and trees planted in every vacant bit of ground.

Last year some 9.2 million persons came to the Nation's Capital and spent a record $410 million, according to the Washington Convention and Visitors Bureau.

Lord Lister

Celebrating Lord Joseph Lister & Luther Leonidas Hill: The Washington branch of the English-Speaking Union celebrated the Centennial of the birth of Lord Joseph Lister on October 14, 1965 at the Washington Hilton Hotel. The speaker for the occasion, Sir Charles Illingworth, CBE, Regius Professor Emeritus of Surgery, University of Glasgow, Scotland spoke on "Lister's Legacy to Humanity."

The President of the English-Speaking Union, Mr. Edward Russell, introduced all the guests seated at the head table. Among those introduced were Mrs. Russell; Dr. Henry A. Darner; Gov. Alfred A. Driscoll of New Jersey; Mrs. Robert Sargent Shriver; former Vice President Nixon; Mrs. Maurice Morris; and Lister and me. Around four hundred guests assembled.

Each guest received a souvenir program that included a biographical sketch of Lord Lister's life. To quote from the sketch, "In an age which everyone knows about the dangers of infected wounds, few will dispute this tribute by a biographer to the discovery of antisepsis. Most people too will find it hard to believe that this discovery was made only one hundred years ago, and that up to that time the world of surgery was haunted by the usually fatal operation infection."

Queen Victoria elevated Joseph Lister to the peerage in 1879. Lister's death came at an advanced age in 1912. Parliament wished to have him buried in Westminster Abbey but Lister declined the honor as he wished to be buried by his beloved wife Agnes.

Eight years ago, Lister and I were in England for a short visit. We drove out to the Hampstead Cemetery, which is only a short distance from London, to pay our respects to one of the world's greatest surgeons, Joseph Lister. His tombstone, a small inconspicuous marker, was placed beside that of his wife Agnes, as he had requested.

Dr. L.L. Hill, a pupil of Joseph Lister, and Senator Lister Hill (the namesake of this great doctor) make an interesting trio in the field of medicine—and in the health of the world.

Dr. L.L. Hill studied medicine at New York Medical College in Philadelphia. He interned at New York Polyclinic Hospital. In 1883 he went to England to study under Joseph Lister.

When Dr. Hill went back to practice medicine in his home town of Montgomery, Alabama, he found most of his colleagues in opposition to the revolutionary methods which he had learned from Joseph Lister. Finally when it was proven that the use of antisepsis saved lives, other doctors began adopting these methods with the same success.

At the birth of his son Lister on December 29, 1894, Dr. Hill wrote his teacher to inform him that he had named the boy for him. In reply Dr. Lister wrote these words: "I wish for my namesake a life of health, goodness, and usefulness."

The boy Lister tried being a doctor for a day, but gave up the idea after watching a bloody operation that his father performed. Later that day, the young Lister admitted, "Father, I don't want to be a doctor."

I feel certain that Lord Lister, and Dr. Hill, would both be very pleased at the contribution Senator Hill has made in the field of medicine, medical research, in the education and training of doctors, dentists, and other health personnel, and in the construction of hospitals and other health facilities.

I think it is required of a man that he should share the action and passions of his times at peril of being judged not to have lived.

~